MASTER THE™ DSST®

Foundations
of Education
Exam

About Peterson's

Peterson's® has been your trusted educational publisher for more than 50 years. It's a milestone we're quite proud of, as we continue to offer the most accurate, dependable, high-quality educational content in the field, providing you with everything you need to succeed. No matter where you are on your academic or professional path, you can rely on Peterson's for our books, online information, expert test-prep tools, the most up-to-date education exploration data, and the highest quality career success resources—everything you need to achieve your education goals. For our complete line of products, visit **www.petersons.com.**

For more information, contact Peterson's, 4380 S. Syracuse Street, Suite 200, Denver CO 80237; 800-338-3282 Ext. 54229; or visit us online at **www.petersons.com**.

ISBN-13: 978-0-7689-4448-8

Printed in the United States of America

10 9 8 7 6 5 4 3 2 1   23 22 21

Contents

Before You Begin

HOW THIS BOOK IS ORGANIZED

Peterson's *Master the*™ *DSST*® *Introduction to Foundations of Education Exam* provides a diagnostic test, subject-matter review, and a post-test.

- **Diagnostic Test**—Twenty multiple-choice questions, followed by an answer key with detailed answer explanations
- **Assessment Grid**—A chart designed to help you identify areas that you need to focus on based on your test results
- **Subject-Matter Review**—General overview of the exam subject, followed by a review of the relevant topics and terminology covered on the exam
- **Post-test**—Sixty multiple-choice questions, followed by an answer key and detailed answer explanations

The purpose of the diagnostic test is to help you figure out what you know—or don't know. The twenty multiple-choice questions are similar to the ones found on the DSST exam, and they should provide you with a good idea of what to expect. Once you take the diagnostic test, check your answers to see how you did. Included with each correct answer is a brief explanation regarding why a specific answer is correct, and in many cases, why other options are incorrect. Use the assessment grid to identify the questions you miss so that you can spend more time reviewing that information later. As with any exam, knowing your weak spots greatly improves your chances of success.

Following the diagnostic test is a subject-matter review. The review summarizes the various topics covered on the DSST exam. Key terms are defined; important concepts are explained; and when appropriate, examples are provided. As you read the review, some of the information may seem familiar while other information may seem foreign. Again, take note of the unfamiliar because that will most likely cause you problems on the actual exam.

After studying the subject-matter review, you should be ready for the post-test. The post-test contains sixty multiple-choice items, and it will serve as a dry run for the real DSST exam. There are complete answer explanations at the end of the test.

OTHER DSST® PRODUCTS BY PETERSON'S

Books, flashcards, practice tests, and videos available online at **www.petersons.com/testprep/dsst**

- A History of the Vietnam War
- Art of the Western World
- Astronomy
- Business Mathematics
- Business Ethics and Society
- Civil War and Reconstruction
- Computing and Information Technology
- Criminal Justice
- Environmental Science
- Ethics in America
- Ethics in Technology
- Foundations of Education
- Fundamentals of College Algebra
- Fundamentals of Counseling
- Fundamentals of Cybersecurity
- General Anthropology
- Health and Human Development
- History of the Soviet Union
- Human Resource Management
- Introduction to Business
- Introduction to Geography
- Introduction to Geology
- Introduction to Law Enforcement
- Introduction to World Religions
- Lifespan Developmental Psychology
- Math for Liberal Arts
- Management Information Systems
- Money and Banking
- Organizational Behavior
- Personal Finance
- Principles of Advanced English Composition
- Principles of Finance
- Principles of Public Speaking
- Principles of Statistics
- Principles of Supervision
- Substance Abuse
- Technical Writing

Like what you see? Get unlimited access to Peterson's full catalog of DSST practice tests, instructional videos, flashcards, and more for **75% off the first month!** Go to **www.petersons.com/testprep/dsst** and use coupon code **DSST2020** at checkout. Offer expires July 1, 2021.

Chapter 1

All About the DSST® Exam

WHAT IS DSST®?

Previously known as the DANTES Subject Standardized Tests, the DSST program provides the opportunity for individuals to earn college credit for what they have learned outside of the traditional classroom. Accepted or administered at more than 1,900 colleges and universities nationwide and approved by the American Council on Education (ACE), the DSST program enables individuals to use the knowledge they have acquired outside the classroom to accomplish their educational and professional goals.

WHY TAKE A DSST® EXAM?

DSST exams offer a way for you to save both time and money in your quest for a college education. Why enroll in a college course in a subject you already understand? For more than 30 years, the DSST program has offered the perfect solution for individuals who are knowledgeable in a specific subject and want to save both time and money. A passing score on a DSST exam provides physical evidence to universities of proficiency in a specific subject. More than 1,900 accredited and respected colleges and universities across the nation award undergraduate credit for passing scores on DSST exams. With the DSST program, individuals can shave months off the time it takes to earn a degree.

The DSST program offers numerous advantages for individuals in all stages of their educational development:

- Adult learners
- College students
- Military personnel

Adult learners desiring college degrees face unique circumstances—demanding work schedules, family responsibilities, and tight budgets. Yet adult learners also have years of valuable work experience that can frequently be applied toward a degree through the DSST program. For example, adult learners with on-the-job experience in business and management might be able to skip the Business 101 courses if they earn passing marks on DSST exams such as Introduction to Business and Principles of Supervision.

Adult learners can put their prior learning into action and move forward with more advanced course work. Adults who have never enrolled in a college course may feel a little uncertain about their abilities. If this describes your situation, then sign up for a DSST exam and see how you do. A passing score may be the boost you need to realize your dream of earning a degree. With family and work commitments, adult learners often feel they lack the time to attend college. The DSST program provides adult learners with the unique opportunity to work toward college degrees without the time constraints of semester-long course work. DSST exams take two hours or less to complete. In one weekend, you could earn credit for multiple college courses.

The DSST exams also benefit students who are already enrolled in a college or university. With college tuition costs on the rise, most students face financial challenges. The fee for each DSST exam starts at $85 (plus administration fees charged by some testing facilities)—significantly less than the $750 average cost of a 3-hour college class. Maximize tuition assistance by taking DSST exams for introductory or mandatory course work. Once you earn a passing score on a DSST exam, you are free to move on to higher-level course work in that subject matter, take desired electives, or focus on courses in a chosen major.

Not only do college students and adult learners profit from DSST exams, but military personnel reap the benefits as well. If you are a member of the armed services at home or abroad, you can initiate your post-military career by taking DSST exams in areas with which you have experience. Military personnel can gain credit anywhere in the world, thanks to the fact that almost all of the tests are available through the internet at designated testing locations. DSST testing facilities are located at more than 500 military installations, so service members on active duty can get a jump-start on a post-military career with the DSST program. As an additional incentive, DANTES (Defense Activity for Non-Traditional Education Support) provides funding for DSST test fees for eligible members of the military.

More than 30 subject-matter tests are available in the fields of Business, Humanities, Math, Physical Science, Social Sciences, and Technology.

Available DSST® Exams

Business	Social Sciences
Business Ethics and Society	A History of the Vietnam War
Business Mathematics	Art of the Western World
Computing and Information Technology	Criminal Justice
Human Resource Management	Foundations of Education
Introduction to Business	Fundamentals of Counseling
Management Information Systems	General Anthropology
Money and Banking	History of the Soviet Union
Organizational Behavior	Introduction to Geography
Personal Finance	Introduction to Law Enforcement
Principles of Finance	Lifespan Developmental Psychology
Principles of Supervision	Substance Abuse
	The Civil War and Reconstruction
Humanities	**Physical Sciences**
Ethics in America	Astronomy
Introduction to World Religions	Environmental Science
Principles of Advanced English Composition	Health and Human Development
Principles of Public Speaking	Introduction to Geology
Math	**Technology**
Fundamentals of College Algebra	Ethics in Technology
Math for Liberal Arts	Fundamentals of Cybersecurity
Principles of Statistics	Technical Writing

As you can see from the table, the DSST program covers a wide variety of subjects. However, it is important to ask two questions before registering for a DSST exam.

1. Which universities or colleges award credit for passing DSST exams?
2. Which DSST exams are the most relevant to my desired degree and my experience?

Knowing which universities offer DSST credit is important. In all likelihood, a college in your area awards credit for DSST exams, but find out before taking an exam by contacting the university directly. Then review the list of DSST exams to determine which ones are most relevant to the degree you are seeking and to your base of knowledge. Schedule an appointment with your college adviser to determine which exams best fit your degree program and which college courses the DSST exams can replace. Advisers should also be able to tell you the minimum score required on the DSST exam to receive university credit.

DSST® TEST CENTERS

You can find DSST testing locations in community colleges and universities across the country. Check the DSST website (**www.getcollegecredit. com**) for a location near you or contact your local college or university to find out if the school administers DSST exams. Keep in mind that some universities and colleges administer DSST exams only to enrolled students. DSST testing is available to men and women in the armed services at more than 500 military installations around the world.

HOW TO REGISTER FOR A DSST® EXAM

Once you have located a nearby DSST testing facility, you need to contact the testing center to find out the exam administration schedule. Many centers are set up to administer tests via the internet, while others use printed materials. Almost all DSST exams are available as online tests, but the method used depends on the testing center. The cost for each DSST exam starts at $85, and many testing locations charge a fee to cover their costs for administering the tests. Credit cards are the only accepted payment method for taking online DSST exams. Credit card, certified check, and money order are acceptable payment methods for paper-and-pencil tests.

Test takers are allotted two score reports—one mailed to them and another mailed to a designated college or university, if requested. Online tests generate unofficial scores at the end of the test session, while individuals taking paper tests must wait four to six weeks for score reports.

PREPARING FOR A DSST® EXAM

Even though you are knowledgeable in a certain subject matter, you should still prepare for the test to ensure you achieve the highest score possible. The first step in studying for a DSST exam is to find out what will be on the specific test you have chosen. Information regarding test content is located on the DSST fact sheets, which can be downloaded at no cost from **www.getcollegecredit.com**. Each fact sheet outlines the topics covered on a subject-matter test, as well as the approximate percentage assigned to each topic. For example, questions on the Foundations of Education exam are distributed in the following way: Contemporary Issues in Education—50%; Past and Current Influences on Education—30%; and Interrelationships between Contemporary Issues and Influences, Past or Current, in Education—20%.

In addition to the breakdown of topics on a DSST exam, the fact sheet also lists recommended reference materials. If you do not own the recommended books, then check college bookstores. Avoid paying high prices for new textbooks by looking online for used textbooks. Don't panic if you are unable to locate a specific textbook listed on the fact sheet; the textbooks are merely recommendations. Instead, search for comparable books used in university courses on the specific subject. Current editions are ideal, and it is a good idea to use at least two references when studying for a DSST exam. Of course, the subject matter provided in this book will be a sufficient review for most test takers. However, if you need additional information, then it is a good idea to have some of the reference materials at your disposal when preparing for a DSST exam.

Fact sheets include other useful information in addition to a list of reference materials and topics. Each fact sheet includes subject-specific sample questions like those you will encounter on the DSST exam. The sample questions provide an idea of the types of questions you can expect on the exam. Test questions are multiple-choice with one correct answer and three incorrect choices.

The fact sheet also includes information about the number of credit hours ACE has recommended be awarded by colleges for a passing DSST exam score. However, you should keep in mind that not all universities and colleges adhere to the ACE recommendation for DSST credit hours. Some institutions require DSST exam scores higher than the minimum score recommended by ACE. Once you have acquired appropriate reference materials and you have the outline provided on the fact sheet, you are ready to start studying, which is where this book can help.

TEST DAY

After reviewing the material and taking practice tests, you are finally ready to take your DSST exam. Follow these tips for a successful test day experience.

1. **Arrive on time.** Not only is it courteous to arrive on time to the DSST testing facility, but it also allows plenty of time for you to take care of check-in procedures and settle into your surroundings.

2. **Bring identification.** DSST test facilities require that candidates bring a valid government-issued identification card with a current photo and signature. Acceptable forms of identification include a current driver's license, passport, military identification card, or state-issued identification card. Individuals who fail to bring proper identification to the DSST testing facility will not be allowed to take an exam.

3. **Bring the right supplies.** If your exam requires the use of a calculator, you may bring a calculator that meets the specifications. For paper-based exams, you may also bring No. 2 pencils with an eraser and black ballpoint pens. Regardless of the exam methodology, you are NOT allowed to bring reference or study materials, scratch paper, or electronics such as cell phones, personal handheld devices, cameras, alarm wrist watches, or tape recorders to the testing center.

4. **Take the test.** During the exam, take the time to read each question-and-answer option carefully. Eliminate the choices you know are incorrect to narrow the number of potential answers. If a question completely stumps you, take an educated guess and move on—remember that DSSTs are timed; you will have 2 hours to take the exam.

With the proper preparation, DSST exams will save you both time and money. So join the thousands of people who have already reaped the benefits of DSST exams and move closer than ever to your college degree.

FOUNDATIONS OF EDUCATION EXAM FACTS

The DSST® Foundations of Education exam consists of 100 multiple-choice questions that assess students for knowledge equivalent to that acquired in a Foundations of Education college course. The exam includes the following topics: Contemporary issues in education; past and current influences on education; and interrelationships between contemporary issues and influences.

Area or Course Equivalent: Foundations of Education
Level: Lower-level baccalaureate
Amount of Credit: 3 Semester Hours
Minimum Score: 400
Source: https://www.getcollegecredit.com/wp-content/assets/factsheets/FoundationsOfEducation.pdf

I. **Contemporary Issues in Education – 50%**

    a. Equity

    b. Governance

    c. Curriculum

    d. Professional issues

    e. Technology issues

II. **Past and Current Influences on Education – 30%**

    a. Philosophies, theories, ideologies

    b. Democratic ideals

    c. Social/Economic influences

III. **Interrelationships between Contemporary Issues and Influences, Past or Current, in Education – 20%**

    a. Tradition and progress

    b. National versus local control

    c. Secular versus religious

    d. Civil rights

    e. Public versus private

Chapter 2

Foundations of Education Diagnostic Test

DIAGNOSTIC TEST ANSWER SHEET

1. Ⓐ Ⓑ Ⓒ Ⓓ	8. Ⓐ Ⓑ Ⓒ Ⓓ	15. Ⓐ Ⓑ Ⓒ Ⓓ
2. Ⓐ Ⓑ Ⓒ Ⓓ	9. Ⓐ Ⓑ Ⓒ Ⓓ	16. Ⓐ Ⓑ Ⓒ Ⓓ
3. Ⓐ Ⓑ Ⓒ Ⓓ	10. Ⓐ Ⓑ Ⓒ Ⓓ	17. Ⓐ Ⓑ Ⓒ Ⓓ
4. Ⓐ Ⓑ Ⓒ Ⓓ	11. Ⓐ Ⓑ Ⓒ Ⓓ	18. Ⓐ Ⓑ Ⓒ Ⓓ
5. Ⓐ Ⓑ Ⓒ Ⓓ	12. Ⓐ Ⓑ Ⓒ Ⓓ	19. Ⓐ Ⓑ Ⓒ Ⓓ
6. Ⓐ Ⓑ Ⓒ Ⓓ	13. Ⓐ Ⓑ Ⓒ Ⓓ	20. Ⓐ Ⓑ Ⓒ Ⓓ
7. Ⓐ Ⓑ Ⓒ Ⓓ	14. Ⓐ Ⓑ Ⓒ Ⓓ	

FOUNDATIONS OF EDUCATION DIAGNOSTIC TEST
24 minutes—20 questions

Directions: Carefully read each of the following 20 questions. Choose the best answer to each question and fill in the corresponding circle on the answer sheet. The Answer Key and Explanations can be found following this Diagnostic Test.

1. How does the US Constitution address the issue of education in America?

    A. It explicitly delegates the matter to the states.
    B. It is silent on the matter of education.
    C. It established the US Department of Education but allowed states to exercise control.
    D. It established the US Department of Education that controls all matters pertaining to education.

2. Planned experiences provided via instruction through which schools meet their goals and objectives are known as

    A. adequate yearly progress.
    B. curriculum.
    C. individualized education programs.
    D. student experience.

3. The landmark decision determining that "separate but equal" facilities were, in fact, inherently unequal, was

    A. *Brown v. Board of Education.*
    B. *Plessy v. Ferguson.*
    C. *Dred Scott v. Sanford.*
    D. *Loving v. Virginia.*

4. *Middletown*, a report on the sociology of a fictional city (in reality, Muncie, IN), described

    A. the relationship between social class and achievement in school.
    B. the effects of pollution on educational achievement.
    C. the effects of the introduction of new technologies in schools.
    D. the effects of unionism and collective bargaining on education.

5. Equity in education is generally defined as

 A. accessibility for all students.
 B. equal treatment for all students regardless of gender, race, or disability.
 C. equal access to all educational resources, opportunities, and experiences needed for success.
 D. treating all students the same.

6. _____ schools champion the idea that teaching should be "open-ended" and geared to the pace at which each student learns.

 A. Waldorf
 B. Charter
 C. Magnet
 D. Montessori

7. The Common Core State Standards have been

 A. adopted by a minority of US states.
 B. nullified by most state legislatures.
 C. adopted by all US states and protectorates.
 D. adopted by a majority of US states.

8. For several reasons, many do not consider teaching to be an actual profession and tend not to regard teachers as professionals. Their reluctance is based on the absence of one or more hallmarks of professionalism, which include the following: 1) a defined and agreed-upon body of knowledge, 2) control over licensing standards and entry requirements, and 3) high prestige and economic standing. Which one of the following is an additional reason that teaching is often not considered a profession?

 A. The presence of union activities in schools
 B. Adherence to a school- or district-wide dress code
 C. Autonomy in decision-making about certain areas of work
 D. Degree requirements

9. Dewey and other progressives sought to replace Spencer's ideas on competition with an emphasis on

   A. the law of the jungle.
   B. science and technology.
   C. cooperation.
   D. study of the classics.

10. In 1996, the US government embraced technology by releasing the first nationwide comprehensive educational technology plan, *Getting Students Ready for the Twenty-First Century: Meeting the Technology Literacy Challenge*. The plan was mainly aimed at

    A. getting computers and internet into the classroom.
    B. combatting technological illiteracy.
    C. providing laptop computers to schools, so that students could take them home.
    D. teaching programming as a means of securing post-graduation employment.

11. A "dame school" was

    A. a school established to teach young girls the basics of homemaking.
    B. a private school taught by a woman, often in her home, and open to young girls and boys.
    C. a name for any small college that catered to wealthy young women.
    D. a school for boys, but with mostly female teachers.

12. The CEO of a school district is

    A. the principal.
    B. the superintendent.
    C. the chairman of the school board.
    D. the mayor of the city in which the district is located.

13. The strict requirements of the No Child Left Behind Act led some teachers and schools to

I. appeal for waivers from some of the requirements.

II. cheat, in order to boost students' test scores.

III. "teach to the test," largely ignoring untested areas of study.

A. I and II
B. II and III
C. I and III
D. I, II, and III

14. Educational philosophies existed long before the establishment of the United States. More than one early approach stressed listening, memorization, recitation, and commentary on sacred texts as a means of inculcating beliefs and ideals and passing those on from one generation to the next. While much of this approach has been adopted (and then abandoned and then adopted again) by the contemporary establishment, some aspects have proven to be controversial. What aspects are those?

A. Inculcating and passing on cultural beliefs
B. The teaching of religion
C. Rote memorization
D. All of the above.

15. Which of the following might be considered a negative effect of the use of technology?

A. Using social networking and email to connect with classrooms around the world
B. Extending classroom experiences by using social networks
C. Encouragement of social isolation
D. Providing rich media sources of information

16. The newest teacher-preparation accreditation body, the CAEP (Council for the Accreditation of Educator Preparation, fully established in 2013), utilizes peer review and evidence-based accreditation in an effort to evaluate teacher-preparation programs. What were the two predecessors of CAEP?

    A. NCATE and TEAC
    B. NCTE and TEAC
    C. TEAC and CAEP
    D. TEAC and NEA

17. Which of the following is true about gender-related differences in educational achievement?

    A. They are slowly disappearing.
    B. They no longer exist.
    C. They have increased over the past 15 years.
    D. They have remained the same over the past decade.

18. Title IX of the 1972 United States Education Amendments prohibited sexual discrimination in federally funded school activities. This included athletics, but that was not the only area of impact. Which of the following is true?

    A. Prior to the passage of Title IX, it was legal to expel a student if she were pregnant.
    B. Title IX ensures that male and female athletic programs must be identical.
    C. Title IX requires that anyone, male or female, must be allowed to play on a "boys'" football, baseball, or other team.
    D. Title IX does not require that males and females have equal locker room facilities.

19. A school board is a group of elected or appointed citizens who set policy for local schools. The majority of school board members

    A. are paid for their services.
    B. come from the education profession.
    C. serve as unpaid volunteers.
    D. are appointed rather than elected.

20. In response to the perceived Protestant leanings of the nineteenth century public schools of the time,

    A. the state governments forbade schools from using prayers and Bible readings in class.
    B. Catholic immigrants created their own system of parochial schools.
    C. German immigrants created their own Lutheran schools.
    D. the federal government sued the state governments for breaching the First Amendment's "Establishment" and "Free Exercise" clauses.

ANSWER KEY AND EXPLANATIONS

1. B	5. C	9. C	13. D	17. A
2. B	6. D	10. B	14. D	18. A
3. A	7. D	11. B	15. C	19. C
4. A	8. C	12. B	16. A	20. B

1. **The correct answer is B.** The Constitution says nothing about education. Consistent with the Tenth Amendment's reserved powers clause, the states have taken that silence to mean that the federal government has delegated control of education to the individual states. The Constitution does not explicitly delegate the matter to the states (choice A), but its silence on the matter implies that it is one of those powers reserved to the states. Choices C and D are incorrect because the Constitution did not establish the Department of Education. The department was created as a noncabinet-level agency in 1867 to collect information about schools and to offer the states help in establishing effective school systems. It was immediately criticized as having the potential to usurp local control of the schools and was reduced to a staff of four and a budget of $15,000. The Department of Education does not control all matters pertaining to education, which are still under state control, except for those issues affected by federal funding. The federal government's share of funding is about 8%.

2. **The correct answer is B.** Curriculum encompasses those planned experiences that occur via instruction as schools work to achieve their educational goals and objectives. Adequate yearly progress (choice A) is a measurement of progress that was required by the No Child Left Behind Act before it was replaced by the Every Student Succeeds Act (ESSA). An Individualized Education Program (choice C) is a document developed for children who require special education. Student experience (choice D) is a catch-all term that tends to be used as marketing-speak to refer to post-secondary students' overall school experience, positive or negative. If a post-secondary institution is considered as a business (and they often are), then measures of "the student experience" are tools meant to boost retention or possibly to explain a lack of retention.

3. The correct answer is A. *Brown v. Board of Education* (1954) determined that an earlier decision (in *Plessy v. Ferguson*) was unconstitutional and affirmed that "separate but equal" facilities were inherently unequal. The *Plessy* decision (choice B) in 1896 originally affirmed that the use of "separate but equal" facilities were allowed. This would be overturned by *Brown* almost 60 years later. The *Dred Scott* decision (choice C) denied citizenship (and basic rights accruing from citizenship) to all blacks—free or enslaved. In *Loving v. Virginia* (choice D), the Supreme Court determined (in 1967) that state laws prohibiting interracial marriage were unconstitutional.

4. The correct answer is A. The 1937 study concluded that parents recognize the importance of education for their children, but that many working-class children came to school unprepared to acquire the skills required for success in the classroom. Many subsequent studies have shown that there is a close relationship between social class and education in the United States. The other choices refer to topics that have been the subject of studies, but not the *Middletown* report.

5. The correct answer is C. Equity exists when all students are provided the same opportunities for success. Choice A is incorrect because equity in education presumes—but is not limited to—provisions for accessibility and accommodation to special needs. Providing equal treatment for all students (choice B) is not enough; some students have special needs or circumstances. Treating every student the same (choice D) assumes that each student has the same background, abilities, and needs. As one researcher has said, ". . . equality is not enough to combat hundreds of years of oppression, poverty, and disproportionality."

6. **The correct answer is D.** In a Montessori school, the curriculum is open-ended, and each student learns at his or her own pace. In a Waldorf school (choice A), the curriculum may be specific, but disciplines are tied together as much as possible. The result is that subjects tend to be studied not in isolation, but in relation to other subjects. Teachers in a Waldorf school have a great deal of leeway in determining *how* the curriculum will be taught and what activities might be used to cover that curriculum, but the curriculum itself is prescribed. Charter schools (choice B) are public schools set up under community control to provide alternative visions of schooling. Charter schools have more autonomy from state and district regulations, including the freedom to design their own curriculum. Magnet schools (choice C) are public schools with an emphasis on specialized curricula; these are often set up in an effort to attract students throughout a school district, sometimes in an effort to encourage desegregation.

7. **The correct answer is D.** Over 40 states (plus the District of Columbia), a sizable majority, have adopted the Common Core State Standards. Under ESSA, the federal government can no longer *mandate* their adoption.

8. **The correct answer is C.** It is the belief of some that to be considered a professional, one must exercise a certain degree of autonomy in one's work, which is thought to be lacking in teaching. Instead, teachers are often told what, when, where, and how to teach. Neither the presence of union activities (choice A) nor the fact that a degree is required (choice D) are reasons that teaching is not considered a profession. The presence of a school dress code (choice B) is not considered one of the reasons, though some might feel that it is demeaning or restrictive.

9. **The correct answer is C.** While Spencer emphasized a social Darwinist mindset that relied on competition to bring out the best (and to lift up the fittest among us), Dewey and many other progressives championed cooperation and collaboration in the classroom. The "law of the jungle" (choice A) is just another way of saying "survival of the fittest," which was Spencer's Darwinist creed. Spencer, not Dewey, emphasized science and technology (choice B) in his curriculum, because he felt that the best education was a utilitarian one; the progressives would not have wanted to replace a Spencerian curriculum with yet another Spencerian curriculum. Many perennialists touted a study of the classics (choice D) as the best basis for a curriculum. Dewey, as a progressive, would not have suggested that as a replacement for Spencer's social Darwinism.

10. **The correct answer is B.** Having noted that technology literacy was a "national priority," the main goal was to eliminate technological illiteracy. In service of that goal, the plan recommended getting computers and internet (at the time, the "information superhighway") into the classroom (choice A). There was no plan to get laptops into the hands of students (choice C), at least, not at the federal level. Producing more programmers (choice D) was not a direct goal of the plan.

11. **The correct answer is B.** The dame schools were schools run from a woman's home, in which children were taught the basics: reading, writing, arithmetic, and religion. Since only boys were allowed in many of the higher-level schools (including the common schools), this was often the only formal education that young girls received. Homemaking skills (choice A) were taught only incidentally. There were eventually many small colleges (or "finishing schools") that catered to wealthy young women (choice C), but these were not known as "dame schools." Attendance at dame schools was not restricted to boys (choice D).

12. **The correct answer is B.** The superintendent runs the district, much like a company's chief executive officer runs a company. In fact, while many superintendents are educators, more and more businesspeople and military officers are being hired as school district superintendents. The principal (choice A) runs a specific school—often referred to simply as a "building"—and is in effect the chief administrative officer of the school. The chairman of the school board (choice C) has a great deal of input, but no actual authority except during a board meeting. The mayor of the city (choice D) has no direct authority over the district or the schools within it. In fact, many school districts—Los Angeles Unified, for one—are large enough that they span multiple cities.

13. **The correct answer is D.** The strict requirements of the No Child Left Behind Act resulted in all three responses from teachers and schools.

14. **The correct answer is D.** All of the choices listed are still causing controversy in today's educational environment. Historically, the inculcation of cultural beliefs (choice A) has been part of what schools have done—indeed, what they set out to do. However, that flies in the face of the notion that the country is essentially multicultural, so some have complained that the educational system tends to teach only to the dominant culture and oppresses the others. In the public schools, the teaching of religion (choice B) has been controversial for a number of reasons, including disagreements about which would be the "correct" religion to teach. Even religious studies that give equal treatment to multiple religions have come under fire, perhaps *because* they give equal treatment to several religions. Rote memorization (choice C) has been criticized as ineffective, in addition to the idea that it does not constitute "real" learning—a deeper understanding of the subject being examined.

15. **The correct answer is C.** Ironically, some of the technologies meant to help connect people can also work to isolate. This can be especially true of social networks that connect groups of people with similar interests, causing the formation of cliques that serve to ostracize (or even attack) others. Reports of online bullying, intentional "trolling" (i.e., stalking users and leaving hurtful, negative comments), and the spread of gossip or hoaxes from actual news are on the rise. Younger children who lack the ability to differentiate real, meaningful, and useful communications from peer pressure are especially at risk for isolation. The other choices all represent positive uses of technology.

16. **The correct answer is A.** The NCATE (National Council for the Accreditation of Teacher Education) and TEAC (the Teacher Education Accreditation Council) are predecessors to CAEP, which has adopted standards that attempt to determine which teacher-education programs comply with national standards. Neither the National Council of Teachers of English (NCTE) nor the National Education Association (NEA) are considered predecessors.

17. **The correct answer is A.** Gender-based differences are disappearing, though slowly. For example, although boys have traditionally been thought to be higher achievers in math and science, recent research suggests that girls constitute a growing percentage of the highest-achieving students in mathematics and higher order thinking. To say that gender-related differences do not exist is not accurate, so choice B cannot be correct. The differences have decreased, not increased as choice C erroneously indicates. The differences between the genders in educational achievement are slowly disappearing, not remaining static as choice D indicates.

18. **The correct answer is A.** Before Title IX, it was legal to expel a student who became pregnant. Now schools are prohibited from excluding a pregnant student "from participating in any part of an educational program." Further, the school may not exclude the student from any extracurricular activities. The programs need not be identical (choice B), but they must be equivalent. For example, the girls may field a softball team while the boys field a baseball team, but treatment of the two must be equal, including facilities and opportunities for exposure and practice. The law does not require that girls be allowed to play on boys' teams (choice C) when the sport involved is a contact sport: boxing, wrestling, rugby, ice hockey, football, basketball, and "other sports the purpose or major activity of which involves bodily contact." However, the school may allow participation under certain circumstances. Title IX *does* require that male and female athletes have equal locker room facilities (choice D). For years, it was not uncommon for female athletes to be relegated to second-class facilities, but since 1972, that is illegal, assuming that federal funds are involved. Facilities must be equivalent in all respects, and that includes "locker rooms, practice and competitive facilities."

19. **The correct answer is C.** Few school board members are paid for their time, thereby eliminating choice A. In most cases, their work is done as a volunteer service to the community. Very few school board members come from the education profession as choice B erroneously indicates. Choice D is also incorrect because few school boards are appointed; the vast majority are elected. Critics claim this appointment system leads to too much politics; others claim that election makes the members more accountable to the public.

20. **The correct answer is B.** The system of Catholic private schools began largely as a reaction to the perception that public schools, by including King James Version Bible readings in class, were emphasizing a Protestant orientation. Choice A is incorrect because the state did not forbid prayers and Bible readings in class. No doubt some German immigrants did start their own Lutheran schools as choice C indicates, but it was not a reaction to perceived Protestant leanings since Lutherans are themselves Protestant. Choice D is not true. The federal government did not sue the states or prohibit the continued use of religion in the schools. The relevant clause in the First Amendment reads: "Congress shall make no law respecting an establishment of religion, or prohibiting the free exercise thereof . . . ," which most equate with Thomas Jefferson's phrase about a "wall of separation between church and state."

DIAGNOSTIC TEST ASSESSMENT GRID

Now that you've completed the diagnostic test and read through the answer explanations, you can use your results to target your studying. Find the question numbers from the diagnostic test that you answered incorrectly and highlight or circle them below. Then focus extra attention on the sections dealing with those topics.

Foundations of Education		
Content Area	**Topic**	**Question #**
Contemporary Issues in Education	• Equity • Governance • Curriculum • Professional Issues • Technology Issues	2, 5, 8, 10, 12, 13, 15, 16, 17, 19
Past and Current Influences on Education	• Philosophies, Theories, and Ideologies • Democratic Ideals • Social/Economic Influences	4, 9, 11, 14, 18
Interrelationships between Contemporary Issues and Influences, Past or Current, in Education	• Tradition and Progress • National vs. Local Control • Secular vs. Religious • Civil Rights • Public vs. Private	1, 3, 6, 7, 20

Chapter 3

Foundations of Education Subject Review

OVERVIEW

- Contemporary Issues in Education
- Past and Current Influences on Education
- Interrelationships Between Contemporary Issues and Influences, Past or Current, in Education
- Summing It Up

CONTEMPORARY ISSUES IN EDUCATION

There is no shortage of issues when it comes to education around the world and in the United States in particular, many of which are serious and have led to heated debate. Though many have their roots in the past, they are all issues that ask essential questions about the system as it exists today. The following sections describe Contemporary Issues in Education, the most significant topic on the DSST Foundations of Education exam, accounting for 50% of the questions.

Equity

In education, equality and equity play essential roles in supporting students in and out of the classroom. First, it is important to distinguish between those two concepts as they are not the same thing, especially in a legal context. Equality guarantees that everyone has equal access to resources. On the other hand, equity is an attempt to guarantee access as related to student needs.

To distinguish between equity and equality, consider the following example: an instructor can give a disabled student the same lecture as another student. Here, access to the material is equal but—especially if one student is hearing impaired—not necessarily equitable. The student without the impairment is afforded a better, more complete educational experience than the hearing-impaired student. Thus, the needs of the latter student are not being met.

For another example, consider the plight of a student who has fallen behind in his or her studies, perhaps partly due to a language barrier. If an instructor treats that student the same as another student—perhaps by giving them the same English-language textbook—the instructor is treating each student equally, but that doesn't necessarily mean that the treatment is equitable. In other words, how valuable is a textbook that a student is unable to read? The student would need an assistive program to improve their language comprehension or an alternative text that offers the same information but in an understandable form.

On a larger scale, consider groups of students whose socioeconomic situations may be the result of historical oppression or poverty. As researchers have pointed out, mere equality may not be enough to undo historical injustice or marginalization; additional resources may be called for in order for the treatment of that student to truly be equitable.

If **equity** means equal access to educational resources, opportunities, and experiences needed to allow a student to succeed, then that need sometimes calls for more than mere equality. Educational programs that attempt to compensate for such disadvantages are called **compensatory education**. Their central premise is that students need to have access to the same resources as every other student, and each student is entitled to have access to the same extent as every other student.

Gender Equity

There are well-documented examples of gender bias in the history of the US, from delayed voting privileges to unequal pay. However, recent decades have shown marked shifts in gender inequity as the culture and economy of the US have changed. The stereotypes that may have led to preferential treatment of men in education and certain fields of study in the past have seen some degree of reversal. While discrepancies are still present in a variety of career fields (notably, STEM) and visible in the male dominance of certain roles in society (leadership positions), gender inequity in many regards has declined. And the changes in the cultural landscape of the US are linked to legal measures in the latter half of the 20th century, specifically within educational institutions.

Title IX of the 1972 Education Amendments Act specifies that federally funded male and female programs must be conducted on an equitable basis, free from gender discrimination. Since the passage of Title IX, no one can be excluded from participation or be subjected to discrimination in any educational activity that is receiving financial assistance. If the activity is receiving federal funding (and most do), it is illegal to discriminate based on gender. Even private schools must abide by Title IX if they receive federal funds.

Something important to note about Title IX is that it does not explicitly mention athletics. It may have had a prominent impact on school athletics, but the law specifically prohibits discrimination in *any* federally funded school program. That not only includes athletics, but many other types of activities such as band, drama, student government, etc. It also means that a pregnant student cannot be expelled simply because she is pregnant. Note that the Supreme Court has ruled that sexual harassment and assault are in fact forms of sexual discrimination and are also covered under Title IX. Of course, harassment and assault are also covered under many other laws and statutes.

NOTE: In April 2017, parents in Red Bluff, California filed a Title IX lawsuit alleging that, although girls represented 52% of the student body, only 38% of athletic opportunities were offered to girls. The complaint noted a number of areas in which facilities for girls' sports were not comparable to those provided for boys' sports, including the softball playing field and practice facility and the basketball facilities. The Red Bluff Joint Union High School District school board settled with parents in November 2017.

Disability Equity

Equity remains an issue in education especially for students who have disabilities. We mentioned earlier that merely providing a disabled student with equal access to education may not be the same thing as providing the student with equitable access.

Passed in 1990, the **Individuals with Disabilities Education Act (IDEA)** ensures that students with disabilities are provided with **Free Appropriate Public Education**, or **FAPE**. *Appropriate* is the key word here. The education students receive must be tailored to their specific needs, with the ultimate goal being to provide children with disabilities the same opportunity for education as every other child receives. Under the law, disabled students are to be provided with an **Individualized Education Program (IEP)**, a document that outlines just how that education will be tailored to their needs.

NOTE: From 1975 to 1990, the Individuals with Disabilities Education Act (IDEA) was known as EHA, the Education for All Handicapped Children Act.

Ensuring that disabled students are treated equitably is no small task. According to the National Center for Educational Statistics (**nces.ed.gov**), nearly 14% of all public school students receive some form of special education service under IDEA in 2018–2019. In the classroom, teachers deal with over a dozen types of disabilities, including learning disabilities, visual impairments, hearing impairments, and autism. By far the most common of these are **learning disabilities**, which include dyslexia, auditory processing disorder, language processing disorder, ADHD, dysgraphia, and others.

Teachers are legally responsible for the well-being of all of their students and taking care of a student with disabilities can require extra diligence. School employees have been found liable for student injuries "that a reasonable person should have been able to foresee," in cases where negligence was alleged. If a student (special needs or not) wanders off because the teacher wasn't paying attention and is somehow injured, the teacher could be found liable.

Governance

In the United States, education is controlled at the state level. The reason that states control education—and why the US doesn't have a nationalized system, such as that in Japan or England—is that the Constitution says nothing about education. Since the Constitution doesn't reserve education-related powers to the federal government, by default, those powers go to the state as a result of the Tenth Amendment. The Tenth Amendment contains the **reserved powers clause**, which says that "powers not delegated to the United States by the Constitution, nor prohibited by it to the States, are reserved to the States respectively, or to the people." Thus, the US has effectively 50 different state-run departments of education, all free (to some extent) to develop, establish, and implement curriculum, assessment, accreditation, and graduation standards.

While the control may be primarily given to each state, states still must comply with federal mandates such as those required by the **1965 Elementary and Secondary Education Act (ESEA)**, which means that the states often legislate with those mandates in mind. If not legislated directly by the legislature, the state may compel the state board of education to set, maintain, and assess such standards and requirements. The state board of education in turn advises the state legislature on educational matters.

Each state has a department of education, although the name of the department may vary. Accordingly, each state also has someone in charge of that department. This person may be called a state superintendent of education, director of education, superintendent of public instruction, or a similar title. In most states, the person in charge is appointed by the governor, but in some states, that person is elected.

Normally, the next lower level of control is the school board, but some smaller areas may have an intermediary state agency called a **regional educational service agency (RESA)**. A RESA is an autonomous, tax-supported public school district positioned in between the local board and the state department of education. It is the only educational entity with full access to public schools to ensure implementation of core educational services and programs to develop and maintain shared resources.

For the most part, school districts are run by school boards, the members of which are usually unpaid and elected to their positions. School boards are quite powerful because the state generally delegates much of the responsibility for day-to-day operation of the district to the board and to the superintendent of the school district. The school board is normally in charge of staffing decisions and personnel management, and it must also handle any collective bargaining issues or address any questions that may arise.

The school district's "CEO" is the **superintendent** of schools. The superintendent runs the district, much like a company's chief executive officer runs the company. In fact, while many superintendents are educators, many others—especially in larger districts—are increasingly drawn from the ranks of businesspeople and military officers. This makes a certain amount of sense: large districts can have budgets in the billions of dollars (e.g., the Los Angeles Unified School District budget is over $7 billion), and the stakeholders—parents, school board members, etc.—want that money handled sensibly. In cases such as this, it may be true that the district is being run more like a business enterprise than an educational one. That's not necessarily a bad thing, if people wish to ensure that money is spent wisely, and that the district runs smoothly. Of course, it would then make sense to have educators holding other high-level administrative offices, such as assistant superintendents, directors of curriculum, and similar positions. Note that the hiring of superintendents doesn't always work out, regardless of their backgrounds: the average tenure of a superintendent in a large urban district is only about three years.

The number of school districts in the US is decreasing. According to NCES, in 1939 there were some 117,000 public school districts. In 2012, there were only about 13,500 districts. What happened? In most cases, the smaller districts consolidated into (or were absorbed by) larger districts. Usually that occurred because it was more economical to run one large district rather than multiple small ones: large districts could take advantage of economies of scale when purchasing equipment or supplies, older buildings could be retired, and redundant office positions could be eliminated. Another reason for consolidation is that enrollment numbers in rural areas have been declining for many years and continue to do so. Thus, multiple rural districts serving fewer and fewer students have been encouraged (and occasionally required) to consolidate or merge.

There is one more key player impacting schools' local control, and that is the **principal**. If the superintendent is the district's CEO, the principal is the chief administrative officer (CAO) of a particular school. He or she handles the day-to-day operations of that school, mentors and advises teachers, communicates with parents, and much more. Increasingly, as standardized assessments are more widely utilized (and as improvements are mandated by the federal or state governments), the principal is also charged with demonstrating improved student performance.

We said earlier that the federal government has left much of the educative decision-making power to the states, but that does not mean that the federal government has no impact on those decisions. First of all, even though the states can make their own rules, they cannot enact legislation that would conflict with the US Constitution. For that matter, the state's rules cannot conflict with state constitutions or court decisions, either.

During the nation's first century and beyond, the federal government passed few education-related laws. As noted, almost everything was (and still is) left up to the state. However, beginning in 1965, that began to change. The ESEA was enacted in that year as part of President Johnson's "war on poverty." The act provides federal funds for a variety of uses, including professional development, instructional materials, and more. Its main intent was to help provide equal access to education, with the ultimate goal of reducing achievement gaps between impoverished students and wealthier ones. This was an early example of the government tying federal funding to equal (and equitable) access to educational experiences. Since then, several other examples of federal legislation have helped shape education across the nation, often by requiring federal mandates to be met in order to qualify for federal funding.

There are many who feel that the federal government, represented by the US Department of Education, a cabinet-level department in the executive branch of the government, has overstepped its bounds and has intruded on state and local agencies. This is especially true in the case of what some see as **unfunded mandates**: federal requirements that state and local agencies perform in a certain fashion, but for which the federal government has provided no (or insufficient) funds. Some see the federal government's **No Child Left Behind Act (NCLB)** and its successor, the **Every Student Succeeds Act (ESSA)**, as examples of unfunded mandates, arguing that the states were not provided with funds—or were not provided with funds quickly enough—to meet the requirements of the Acts.

Curriculum

Before we discuss the many ways in which subjects can be taught, we need to consider *what* will be taught. Separating the two is sometimes difficult. The way an instructor likes to teach may form, in one way or another, the content that is being taught. And what an instructor decides (or is told) to teach may influence how that instructor wishes to teach it. We'll separate these concepts here as best as we can, but keep in mind that there's some overlap in the discussion and a great deal of overlap in the classroom as well.

Going back to the Greek and Roman educators, and even before, people have had opinions about what students should learn. **Curriculum** is defined as the planned experiences provided via instruction through which schools meet their goals and objectives, and it has been the subject of debate for as long as there have been schools. Should the curriculum concentrate on the basics? (And if so, what does that mean? What exactly *is* basic?) Should students be given a step-by-step curriculum to follow as they advance from one grade to another? (Should there even be "grades" in the first place?) Should students perhaps determine their *own* curriculum, based on their interests and past experiences? (In which case, what is the role of the teacher?)

Philosophies

There is a good deal of philosophy surrounding the question of what should be taught in the schools, some of which deals with profound questions about the nature of reality.

One approach has at its core the belief that *ideas* are the only true reality, supporting the notion that reality exists within the mind. This is **idealism**, a Platonic principle that, in the context of education, echoes Plato's view that the aim of education is to develop students' abilities and morals in order to serve society. The idealist curriculum therefore emphasizes subject matter concerned with the mind: history, religion, literature, philosophy, and so on.

Realism, on the other hand, is an Aristotelian perspective, a belief that true reality exists *independent* of the mind; that is, the world of physical objects is what constitutes reality. Aristotle was a student of Plato's, but on this they disagreed. A realistic curriculum might focus on science and mathematics and would tend to be standardized.

A third approach is **pragmatism**. A pragmatist believes that only those things that can be experienced are real, and that reality is constantly changing. A pragmatic curriculum, such as that championed by John Dewey, might tend to emphasize hands-on problem-solving and group projects, with an interdisciplinary curriculum. After all, say pragmatists, this is how the world really works: areas of study are not separated, but connected. Science, art, mathematics, history, and so on are all interrelated, with each influencing and being influenced by the others.

One final philosophy pertaining to curriculum is **existentialism**. Existentialist educators believe that education is about human potential and the quest for personal meaning, and this often means a student-centered curriculum that focuses on creating opportunities for self-actualization.

Not surprisingly, there are other philosophies of curriculum. One could write an entire book on educational philosophy, but most of what we'll cover in this overview and in the practice tests can be traced back to one of these four approaches.

History

Curriculum in early America tended to follow the somewhat rigid beliefs of the first European settlers, many of whom brought their educational systems with them. Thus, in New England, **town schools** were established. These were locally controlled primary schools open to boys and girls from ages six to thirteen. Children were taught reading, writing, and religion (in this case, Protestant religion).

Wealthier young boys might attend a **Latin grammar school**, which aimed to prepare them for college. They studied the classical Latin authors, such as Horace, Virgil, and Cicero, and also some of the Greek authors. This classical education emphasized grammar, logic, and rhetoric as stages of intellectual development—as students focused on developing skills with language, first gathering concepts, then reasoning well, and finally working to persuade.

The college for which the boys in Latin grammar schools were being prepared was, of course, **Harvard**, which had been established in 1636. Harvard was originally meant to prepare young men for leadership positions in the ministry and in politics, and its curriculum included not only the classics but also rhetoric and logic, mathematics, ethics and politics, and astronomy.

Pennsylvania's educational history was a bit different than that of the other colonies. Established in 1681 as a proprietary colony that allowed all forms of worship, the colony's educational establishments were just as progressive as its politics. Populated largely by pacifist Quakers (more formally, the Religious Society of Friends), Pennsylvania schools were open to all children—male, female, black, white, and native.

After **Thomas Jefferson** became governor of Virginia in 1779, he sponsored a liberal education bill in the Virginia legislature. Jefferson felt, as did many others, that the purpose of education was to create a literate society of citizens to serve the country's republic. His bill, which failed to pass, promoted state-sponsored schools that would have been open to both boys and girls (but not to slaves); the state would pay for the first few years of education, during which the children would have studied reading, writing, history, and arithmetic. Jefferson also would have opened schools for the older boys to provide a secondary education. Note that Jefferson insisted on a separation of church and state in his schools; religion, he felt, should not be sponsored by the government.

While Jefferson's bill did not pass, several of its provisions raised issues that would be taken up repeatedly in the ongoing debate over what an education should consist of—and who should pay for it.

One early American educator who had a lasting impact on schools and curricula in the new nation was **Noah Webster**, a lexicographer and schoolteacher from New Hampshire. He eventually became a senator and then secretary of state. Webster designed his famous dictionary such that it reflected American usage, and he wrote his spelling and reading books with that same eye toward the Americanization of immigrants. All three books would go on to influence many generations of American children.

In the first half of the nineteenth century, the **common school** movement took hold. Common schools were open to all (other than slaves, at least in the South), and included an opening prayer, pledge of allegiance, and a basic curriculum that included reading, writing, spelling, history, geography, and arithmetic. Recitation was stressed as a learning tool. Common schools were generally one-room schoolhouses that contained several grades. Even then, some objected to the inclusion of a morning prayer: Catholics objected to the use of the King James Version Bible, which they considered to be influenced by Protestant beliefs. Native Americans objected to the use of *any* Bible in a classroom.

After Noah Webster, the man who most influenced education in early America was **Horace Mann**, a Massachusetts politician and a proponent of common schools. Mann advocated a statewide curriculum and instituted school financing through local property taxes. He argued that wealthy people had an obligation to fund public education as a way of investing in the state and felt that education could act as a social equalizer, allowing those who were intelligent and hardworking enough to climb the social and economic ladder. Like Webster, Mann believed that schools would act to Americanize recent immigrants, providing them with a common, unified culture.

Approaches

One way to sum up an approach to curriculum is to classify it as either subject-based or student-based. A **subject-based curriculum** assumes that the subject represents a body of content educators wish the students to understand, or skills educators wish them to possess. A **student-based curriculum** concerns itself largely with the process of *how* a student develops his or her ability to acquire knowledge, rather than focusing on the knowledge itself. Some educational philosophies tend to stress one over the other, but there's normally not a clear-cut distinction; most teachers incorporate both approaches, though they may emphasize one over the other.

Critics of a subject-based curriculum argue that the approach consists of masses of facts learned in isolation, de-emphasizes the students' contemporary life experiences, and allows little student input. Supporters argue that with a student-based curriculum, important components of the required body of knowledge might be overlooked.

The **"great books" curriculum** is an example of a subject-centered curriculum in which the so-called great ideas of Western civilization are presumed to be representative of what is worth knowing. By studying what is presumably the best that the culture has to offer, the ideas that made the civilization great will be transmitted to younger generations, according to proponents of this approach. This sort of curriculum is one that might be recommended by a **perennialist** educator; it is based on the idea that certain ideas are perennial and deserve to be—in fact, *must* be—communicated to future generations. The curriculum, in this case, can be built around these great works, which serve to transmit universal truths.

Related to the perennialist approach is a similar philosophy called **essentialism**. Essentialist educators favor the development of basic (i.e., essential) skills and knowledge: history, mathematics, science—and now, more recent skills such as computer literacy.

Both of these are subject-centered curricular approaches associated with relatively conservative approaches to education. Those traditional approaches fell out of favor with the growth of **progressivism**—with its emphasis on experiential learning and a focus on the "whole child"—in the 1930s and 1940s, on up to the 1970s and beyond. However, the subject-centered approach has experienced a revival in these more conservative times, beginning in the 1980s.

The **back-to-basics movement** is an essentialist approach and a refutation of the progressivism of earlier decades. The back-to-basics movement, which is seen as something of a precursor to NCLB, has resulted in reform legislation that encouraged statewide minimum-competency testing in order for students to graduate. It has also been criticized as an approach that will suppress students' creativity and encourage conformity. Also, it's been shown that as soon as high-stakes testing enters the picture, teachers begin "teaching to the test." On the other hand, proponents feel that back-to-basics—and the high-stakes exit testing that often accompanies it—show that the schools are being held accountable. Additionally, say supporters, the exams focus the curriculum and ensure that key content is covered, and the data provided by the exams can point out problems that can then be addressed.

Exit testing is a natural outgrowth of our wish to ensure that standards are being met, and that students are, in fact, learning. Many curricula are geared toward college studies and are aligned with college admission standards. The idea is that if students can pass those tests, they are more likely to do well in college. Thus, college admission requirements have exerted a strong nationwide influence on curriculum choices for high schools.

Progressivism, championed by John Dewey and his followers (though he eventually disavowed that term), is an approach to curriculum that centers on the whole child, rather than on the subject matter or the teacher. This philosophy stresses that students must test ideas by experimenting, and that learning itself is rooted in the questions of learners. Compared to perennialism and essentialism, progressivism stresses learning by doing and is an active process, rather than a passive one.

Part of the progressive spirit of the 1930s resulted in a demand for what was called **relevant curriculum**, when reformers complained that the existing curriculum did not reflect the economic and social realities of that tumultuous period. Later reformers took up the banner in the 1960s and 1970s, arguing that the traditional curriculum failed to reflect both changing social conditions and students' personal needs. The debate continues today.

Interestingly, one progressive approach was, somewhat confusingly, called the **core curriculum**. The traditional-sounding core curriculum, which gained popularity in the 1930s and 1940s, championed an integrated approach to learning that uses problem-solving as a primary method of instruction. This is a progressive, interdisciplinary approach to curriculum. This approach, however, is not to be confused with the **new core curriculum**, which is an essentialist viewpoint born out of the 1980s reform movement; it's really a "core subjects" approach that requires students to experience a common body of required subjects. So, the *new* core curriculum is actually a return to the basic essentialist curriculum desired by the proponents of the back-to-basics movement.

The new core curriculum came out of the recommendations of the 1983 report *A Nation at Risk: The Imperative for Educational Reform*, issued by the National Commission on Excellence in Education. The report described students as being inadequately prepared for both work and college and recommended a "core subjects" approach that was essentialist in nature, concentrating on "the basics" and requiring students to experience a common body of required subjects. It was a neoconservative movement in curriculum design and educational assessment that is still with us today.

Some approaches to curriculum seem to have little to do with what traditionalist educators have considered curriculum. **Humanism**, for instance, is a psychological perspective on curriculum that grew out of the work of psychologists Abraham Maslow, Carl Rogers, and Arthur Combs. It argues that curriculum must address affective issues such as self-actualization, as well as moral, aesthetic, and higher domains of thinking. The approach emphasizes student independence and self-direction and argues that schools that stress academic achievement do so not for the students' good but for the benefit of adults.

NOTE: Abraham Maslow, best known for creating Maslow's hierarchy of needs, was an American psychologist and a psychology professor at Alliant International University, Brandeis University, Brooklyn College, New School for Social Research, and Columbia University.

Related to humanism are the **values-centered** educational approaches of the 1970s, which included values clarification exercises in which students studied a situation, investigated the facts, considered possible actions and consequences of the action, and then chose a value that would guide further action. A more recent version of this approach, **character education**, places special emphasis on moral and ethical development, and often delves into such subjects as bullying, acceptance of those who are different than oneself, and building a sense of community.

These progressive takes on curriculum are complemented by what have become known as **social and emotional learning (SEL)** programs that aim to improve students' attitudes about themselves, about others, and about school itself. SEL is aligned to a set of skills that are just as important, say supporters, as academic achievements. These are, after all, skills that are needed to succeed in school, in the workplace, and in relationships. Advocates point out that students who are socially and emotionally competent are in fact better equipped to succeed academically.

Such programs have not been without their detractors. For example, one serious concern about school-based character-education programs designed to instill character and to create ethical citizens is that the character-education component could divert time from the school's academic mission. In addition, some worry that such programs could end up simply being attempts at indoctrination. Nonetheless, polls indicate that the public is very much in favor of schools addressing social and emotional needs in addition to academics.

The committee that published *A Nation at Risk: The Imperative for Educational Reform* felt that too much emphasis had been placed on humanistic and other affective approaches to education, and not nearly enough on academic achievement and productivity. Neither the "whole child" nor the nation, they argued, was well served if the student felt good about himself and was able to relate to others but was incapable of drawing inferences from written materials, lacked intermediate reading skills, and was, in effect, functionally illiterate.

Professional Issues

Most teachers consider themselves professionals, but much of the American public does not, and much of the public's perspective is based on the absence of one or more hallmarks of professionalism. Most sociologists agree that a true professional meets the following standards:

- Works with a defined and agreed-upon body of knowledge
- Exercises control over licensing standards and entry requirements
- Enjoys high prestige and economic standing
- Enjoys a certain amount of autonomy in the work and in decisions about the work
- Abides by an agreed-upon code of ethics

If these truly are the criteria for professionalism, then teachers in America do not meet these standards.

While it may be true that teachers enjoy a certain amount of prestige associated with their jobs, that prestige is not accompanied by a salary that one could say contributes to a high economic standing. The body of knowledge with which teachers work with is hardly well-defined and agreed-upon; instead, it is fragmented, disputed, debated, and seems to change every time political winds shift or a new movement gains traction. Teachers, unless they have become government officials or high-level administrators, exercise no control over licensing standards and entry requirements. They have not been in a position to determine who should or should not become a teacher, even when working within fairly powerful labor unions, such as the **American Federation of Teachers (AFT)** or the **National Education Association (NEA)**. Teachers enjoy only limited autonomy: they are generally told what to teach, when to teach it, and, very often, *how* to teach it. Finally, all professions have—and expect their members to abide by—a code of ethics. While the AFT and NEA each promulgate such a code (or in the case of the AFT, the *need* for such a code), teachers are not required to agree to it, nor are they disciplined by their own organization for failing to abide by it. All of these contribute to the perception that teaching is not a true profession.

That perception may be changing. The fact that teachers and teaching programs are accredited—and that teachers *must* be certified in order to teach in most schools—lends both consistency and an air of professionalism to the role. The newest accreditation body, the **Council for the Accreditation of Educator Preparation (CAEP)**, accredits not teachers, but teacher-education programs. The CAEP replaces both the **National Council for the Accreditation of Teacher Education (NCATE)** and the **Teacher Education Accreditation Council (TEAC)**. Formed at the request of—and with the help of—these older organizations, the CAEP's intent is to help professionalize teaching by applying more rigorous standards to education programs.

The **Interstate New Teacher Assessment and Support Consortium (INTASC)** is another organization that aims to help state education agencies prepare and license teachers. It works to further the ongoing professional development of teachers and promulgates a number of standards aimed at professionalizing instruction. These standards cover the following 10 areas:

1. Learner development
2. Learning differences
3. Learning environments
4. Content knowledge
5. Application of content
6. Assessment
7. Planning for instruction
8. Instructional strategies
9. Professional learning and ethics
10. Leadership and collaboration

In addition, INTASC recommends that teachers encourage feedback from students, colleagues, supervisors, and students' families.

> **NOTE:** A review of the current editions of *Foundations of Education* textbooks reveals that the chapter learning objectives are correlated with these INTASC standards.

Note that some have objected to the INTASC standards, fearing that they might encourage an essentialist viewpoint that controls what and how teachers should teach, excludes more progressive perspectives, and causes teachers to end up "teaching to the test." Whatever the merits of those objections, INTASC is an example of an attempt at professionalizing teaching by standardizing its practice.

Among the many requirements of NCLB (since succeeded by ESSA), was one that required teachers to be "highly qualified" in order to hold their posts. In most cases, that meant that teachers must have a bachelor's degree, full state certification or licensure, and must prove that they know each subject they teach. That was the extent of the NCLB's definition, with any refinements or additions to be left to the individual states—which means, of course, that the requirements may differ from one state to another. In most cases, if one has a master's degree in the subject, then one is considered "highly qualified." Some have objected to this on the basis that, while one may be an expert in, for instance, biology, that may not necessarily mean that one knows how to *teach* biology. However, other certification requirements generally address that issue.

> **NOTE:** Private schools are not required to hire certified teachers, though many do require certification.

If an individual is teaching a subject other than the one in which he or she was certified, that person is "teaching out of license." This happens often. At times, the disparity is obvious—for example, an English teacher could end up teaching the occasional social studies course. Occasionally, though, the disparity is more subtle and can be problematic. As an example, an English teacher could end up teaching English as a Second Language (ESL) English courses. In this case, the teacher is certified in English or Language Arts but may have little ESL experience.

Some argue that performance-related **merit pay** will help professionalize teaching. When available, merit pay is awarded as a **value-added measurement (VAM)**, generally based on student performance on standardized tests. Supporters argue that outstanding students must have had outstanding teachers, and they should be rewarded; that merit pay encourages the teacher to focus on the established curriculum, since that's what the assessments measure; and that merit pay attracts better people to teaching instead of losing them to business or other careers. Detractors argue that factors related to student achievement are so diverse that it's difficult to determine the teacher's contribution. These factors may include home environment, peer group influences, and socioeconomic background. Merit pay opponents say that singling out the teacher's contribution is difficult and is perhaps a simplistic approach.

Other steps toward professionalism include improved staff development, national board certification, and mediated entry. **Mediated entry** is the practice of inducting people into a profession in supervised stages to help them learn how to apply their knowledge and skills. This is why doctors go through a demanding internship and then a residency before they're considered fully qualified. The teaching profession is taking steps toward mediated entry by providing mentors, requiring longer preparation time in college, establishing internships, and pairing experienced teachers with new teachers in team teaching situations. New teachers need this support. The attrition rate among new teachers is high, varying somewhere between 20% and 50%. Although the relatively low salary has an impact, much of that attrition is due to the frustration level of new teachers trying to navigate their first year or two of teaching. The move toward mediated entry is supported both by education reform groups and the major teachers' unions.

Technology Issues

Technology has been present in the classroom for quite some time, though its form and use has changed drastically over the years. In the not too distant past, 16mm films, scuffed filmstrips, and scratchy vinyl audio recordings were the norm in classrooms. Even before that, "Schools of The Air" radio programs debuted in the 1930s, bringing cultural and music-appreciation programs into classrooms. **Alexander J. Stoddard** initiated the National Program in the Use of Television in the Schools in 1957, followed by the Midwest Program on Airborne Television Instruction in 1961, to bring televised instruction to the classroom. This was followed by overhead projectors, classroom mimeographs, and videocassette recorders.

Then came computers, computerized courseware, tablets, and mobile apps. In fact, an entire branch of technology-abetted instruction called **M-Learning** has grown out of the use and popularization of mobile devices. These devices can be quite effective—they're small and relatively inexpensive, and many students already possess at least one mobile device. Not surprisingly, though, there are some problems with using mobile tech in the classroom. If students are using their own devices, compatibility issues may be encountered. Having mobile devices in the hands of students also gives them classroom access to unsavory or inaccurate online sources. And then there is the issue of distraction, both by the technology itself and by the content it displays.

All of these innovations were supposed to "disrupt" teaching by changing the way materials were presented and learned. Some of these innovations were supposed to revolutionize the classroom, and at times, they did. At the very least, each change made learning more interesting, more topical, and more accessible.

As we saw with technology from the 1930s to the 1950s, the use of technology in the classroom is nothing new. Even the chalkboard, dating back to the 1800s, is a technology, which served to make learning (and teaching) easier, as did the invention of the pencil and pen, and the slate and stylus prior, and even the wax tablets used long before that. Wax tablets were used as writing surfaces dating back to the Greeks and Romans; to erase what had been written, one simply heated and smoothed the wax surface.

NOTE: The first blackboards were made of slate and came about in 1801, when a geography teacher in Scotland simply hung a large piece of slate on a classroom wall. Soon classrooms around the world had blackboards made of slate. The "greenboard" was introduced in the 1960s, comprised of a steel plate coated with a porcelain-based enamel. This was considered to be an improvement because chalk powder didn't show as well when erased. In the 1980s, schools began using whiteboards, also called dry-erase boards. The blackboard, greenboard, and whiteboard are all fairly low-tech, but each was an improvement on its predecessor, and each was (and still is) an effective learning and teaching tool.

In a sense, any tool, even something as simple as a pencil, is a form of technology. It is in an educator's nature to seek out technologies that potentially could make teaching more useful, relevant, understandable, and effective. There's no reason that the search for useful tools would—or should—end now. In fact, it is now generally agreed that teachers and the educational system needs to prepare students for a technological, digitally connected world, thus adding an even greater impetus to the use of technology in the classroom.

In 1996, the US government embraced technology by releasing the first nationwide comprehensive educational technology plan, known as *Getting Students Ready for the Twenty-First Century: Meeting the Technology Literacy Challenge*. The plan was aimed mainly at combatting technological illiteracy. In the years since the report was issued, teachers—and the institutions that train them—have been advocating for the use of tech tools, including social media, chat rooms, email, computerized courseware, and media-rich digital presentations. These mediums are known to be effective teaching and learning tools, and they are the tools that most students enjoy using.

In addition, technology has been used to increase accessibility for students with disabilities. **Assistive technologies** are equipment or products that can be used to increase, maintain, or improve the functional capabilities of children and adults with disabilities. They are closely related to **adaptive technologies**, which the US government defines as tools that offer external support that can be used to enhance a person's ability to function, such as advanced voice recognition systems, Braille computer displays, and text-to-speech programs. Technology has helped disabled students acquire the FAPE that is required by law.

These technologies are not without controversy. For example, as useful as they can be, social networks have their downsides. The same technology that connects people and groups can, ironically, serve to isolate and ostracize. The internet, which has democratized information, has also democratized *mis*information, spreading hate, gossip, and hoaxes. Bullying, which used to be limited to school hours or to personal contact in the neighborhood, can be a 24/7 reality; everyone is connected all the time, including bullies and their victims. On the plus side, there's a good deal of research that has shown that using the internet is a much more active affair than passively watching television, and that students on social media actually *are* communicating, learning, and exchanging ideas.

NOTE: As of July 2019, there were over 2.4 billion Facebook accounts. Over 1.5 billion account holders log in daily and are considered active users. Every 60 seconds on Facebook, 510,000 comments are posted. Facebook also includes about 83 million fake profiles.

There's another issue with technology, and it's a significant one: not everyone has it. Or at least, not everyone has the same access to it. There exists a **technology gap** (sometimes called a **digital divide**), a term used to describe the advantage enjoyed by those students who have ready access to technology. Not everyone owns a laptop or desktop computer, and not everyone has at-home access to high-speed internet; lack of such access puts some students at a disadvantage.

The gap is real, meaningful, and measurable, and it correlates—not surprisingly—with wealth. Simply put, the more money the family has, the more likely the student is to have access to a computer and to high-speed internet access. Of course, there are alternatives; schools, libraries, and other institutions often offer free access to such tools. Smart phones have helped to bridge—but not eliminate—the gap. The gap also correlates with geography; urban students have greater access than rural, and much greater access than *remote* rural students.

> **NOTE:** In 2012, 54% of all teachers said that their students had adequate internet access at school, but only 18% said that their students had adequate access at home. Since then, the numbers have changed—especially as smart phones have become more prevalent—but the gap remains.

Of course, even if schools can provide access to technology and bring it into the classroom, this does little good if the teacher doesn't know how to use it, or how to use it to its full advantage. As it happens, most state certification (and professional teacher accreditation) programs require the teacher to have shown competence in various forms of educational technology. But one class can't cover everything, and many teachers are reluctant to use "new to them" technology—such as **clickers** (an audience response system that enables teachers to rapidly collect and analyze student responses to questions during class) or an **ELMO** (a document camera that can project documents and other objects onto a screen or wall)—because they're unsure how the technology works or how to incorporate the technology effectively.

Along with knowing how to use the technology, it's equally important that teachers learn to *integrate* the technology into the classroom, using it in their lesson plans and requiring students to use it in pursuit of specific learning objectives. Computers, the internet, email, and the rest can all be used for in-class research, discussion, group activities, assessment, and more.

Interestingly, there is a connection between digital media, the internet, and several families of progressive educational philosophies. Many educators, including John Dewey, Benjamin Bloom, Maria Montessori, and Jerome Bruner, have advocated for a hands-on, project-based, collaborative approach to education. Computers, social media, digital media, and the internet are the perfect tools to enable that kind of collaborative, project-based educational experience. There's even an international group, **iEARN**—the International Education and Resource Network—that helps teachers by providing collaborative tools and resources.

So, what have been the results of the influx of new technology? The results are inconclusive. Some gains have been noted, but they tend to be small and inconsistent. The main problem is apparently not the technology itself, but, as was intimated above, its integration into the classroom. Technology alone is inconsistent in results without effective and imaginative implementation.

Despite that, technology is not going away, and new technologies mean that more resources, financial and otherwise, will be needed in order to keep up with the students and with the technologies themselves. The classroom has always been a magnet for tech tools, and it will remain so.

PAST AND CURRENT INFLUENCES ON EDUCATION

This topic accounts for 30% of the items on the DSST and deals mostly with the philosophies and theories that have impacted education over the years. It also covers social and economic influences, which sometimes effect—or are affected by—those ideologies.

To begin with, we have Islamic scholars to thank for many of the classic works (especially the works of Aristotle, Euclid, and Hippocrates) that have impacted educational philosophies through the years. These works had been lost to the Western world until Muslims translated them into Arabic and then shared them with the rest of the world. The works became important in Islamic education, and Islam eventually helped reintroduce them to Westerners and to Western education. Thus, when we harken back to Aristotle and others, we owe those Islamic scholars a debt of gratitude.

Philosophies, Theories, and Ideologies

We begin with the **sophists**, a group of itinerant teachers in ancient Greece who emphasized rhetoric and public speaking. The sophists taught that, in the new Greek democracy, power could be gained by learning the art of rhetoric, arguing that whoever spoke most persuasively was in a position to influence both the crowds and the democratic assemblies of the day.

NOTE: Protagoras, Gorgias, Antiphon, Prodicus, and Thrasymachus were probably the most famous sophists, but we know of them only by the writings of their opponents, people such as Plato and Socrates.

Socrates and Plato disagreed with the sophists, accusing them of teaching students to debate regardless of the ethical merits of the positions for which they argued. They accused the sophists of having prestige and power as their ultimate (and only) goals. Socrates and Plato argued instead for moral excellence. Ethical behavior, they felt, was a much more virtuous goal than winning arguments for the sake of power or influence.

To speak of ethics, one branch of philosophy directly impacts teachers, students, and the classroom, is to speak of axiology. **Axiology**, which includes the examination of ethics and aesthetics, is the area of philosophy that examines values issues to proscribe some behaviors and prescribe others. Teachers are exposed every day to behaviors that are either proscribed or prescribed—disallowed or encouraged. Note that axiology presumes that there can be a clear definition of ethical behavior, since its aim is to make judgements about both ethics and aesthetics as a way of determining right from wrong and helping to guide students to make ethical choices. Of course, your definition of an ethical behavior might differ from someone else's, which is why some say that the ethics of a certain behavior are dependent on context and culture. This idea is known as **ethical relativism**.

Dozens of educational theorists have influenced the concepts of education and impacted the way teachers teach today. We'll note a few, but keep in mind that this is not a definitive listing of "everyone who's ever been important in learning theory." This list is, insofar as possible, in chronological order.

- **Socrates** (unknown–399 BC) championed a rigorous dialog-based approach and believed in universal truths that were valid in all places and at all times. He encouraged students to use critical self-examination and reflection to bring the universal truths already present in their minds to consciousness.

The **Socratic method** consisted largely of asking leading questions that forced students to think deeply about life, truth, and justice. This is, in fact, an impressively effective teaching method, and it is still used today.

- **Plato** (428 BC–347 BC) was a Greek philosopher, an idealist who believed that the truth was already in an individual's mind and simply needed to be discovered. Thus, for Plato, the purpose of education was to help students discover the universal truths that were already innately present in each person.

- **Aristotle** (384 BC–322 BC) was a student of Plato's, but he disagreed with him about the nature of reality, which he argued existed *outside* of the human mind. Aristotle was the tutor of Alexander the Great and a proponent of compulsory education for men—but not for women, whom he deemed intellectually inferior to men.

- **Jean-Jacque Rousseau** (1712–1778) was a philosopher who argued that monarchs were *not* divinely empowered to rule; that is, he argued against the so-called divine right of kings. Rousseau applied this notably progressive idealism (more correctly, Romanticism) to education, arguing that raising virtuous, moral children was more important than concentrating on academics. The latter would come, he felt, when the children were ready to consider them and, in the meantime, they should be allowed a great deal of freedom in order to encourage creativity; if they did something wrong or misbehaved, they would learn by virtue of the consequences that befell them. Rousseau, an early Romantic, felt that children were not depraved (as was the common perspective), but completely innocent. Rousseau's Romantic notion of children as innocent, playful sprites very much influenced many of the progressive educators who came later.

- **Maria Montessori** (1870–1952) was an Italian educator who wrote about **pedagogy**, the method and practice of teaching. Montessori was a physician, and as a scientist, she sought to develop new teaching methods that would transform students. This "scientific education," she felt, could change how teachers teach. Her educational method was based on the idea that one could allow children to act freely, so long as they were in an environment that was prepared to meet their needs. Students are allowed to follow their own inclinations and to choose and carry out their own activities at their own pace. The result was what Montessori labeled *spontaneous discipline*—that is, discipline that originates within students, rather than being imposed upon them. Her educational method is still used today in many varied forms.

- **John Dewey** (1859–1952) was a philosopher and educational reformer. He was one of the fathers of **pragmatism**, the idea that only that which can be experienced or observed is real, and that truth, being ever evolving, is whatever can be shown to work. In pursuit of this experience, Dewey prescribed

hands-on learning, or "learning by doing." He also favored heavily collaborative educational experiences and project work, arguing that this was a way
to experience reality and build on it, and that it also reflected the way that
students would have to work in the real world.

- **Abraham Maslow** (1908–1970) was not an educator, but an American
  psychologist who is best known for creating a **hierarchy of needs**. This is a
  theory that one's psychological health is predicated on fulfilling a series of
  increasingly high-level needs, and that the higher needs cannot be addressed
  until the basic ones are met. *Physiological needs*—those things required
  to ensure that one's body and mind are working correctly, such as food,
  water, and sleep, are primary needs. The need for *safety* is one level up from
  physiological needs: one must feel physically safe before one can move up to
  the next level. *Love and belonging* are needs that Maslow placed just above
  safety and physiological needs. *Esteem* is a need that Maslow placed close to
  the very top of his hierarchy, just below self-actualization. Self-esteem is an
  ego or status need; people need to feel respected before they can reach the
  top level, *self-actualization*, which is the realization of one's full potential
  and talents. Note that Maslow's hierarchy has been criticized as being both
  simplistic and culture-dependent.
- **Jean Piaget** (1896–1980) was a Swiss psychologist and educational theorist
  who declared, "only education is capable of saving our societies from possible
  collapse, whether violent, or gradual." Piaget listed four stages of cognitive
  development in children and encouraged educators to keep those stages—and
  their limitations—in mind when teaching. The four stages are:

  1. **Sensorimotor:** From birth to age two, children are essentially egocentric
     and unable to perceive the world from others' viewpoints.
  2. **Preoperational:** From age two to seven, children do not yet understand
     logic and still have trouble perceiving things from another's point of view.
  3. **Concrete operational:** From ages seven to about 11, children begin to
     think logically and are no longer egocentric.
  4. **Formal operational:** From age 11 to about 16 or so, children develop the
     capacity for abstract thought and can think logically; they begin to engage
     in problem solving.

A Piagetian classroom would likely be student-centered and **constructivist** in
nature; that is, it would be based on the idea that the learner constructs his or
her reality. Among other things, constructivism assumes that all knowledge
is constructed from the learner's previous knowledge, so that each new step
or concept builds on a previous one.

- **Robert Maynard Hutchins** (1899–1977) was a perennialist and a former president of the University of Chicago who believed that the best education was one that was "calculated to develop the mind." That is, he believed that education should not be specialized or "preprofessional," nor should it be utilitarian. Instead, it should be calculated to develop the mind of the student—and the way to do that, he said, was to expose students to the great minds of the past through the great books. This eventually gave rise to the "great books" curriculum.

- **Alexander S. Neill** (1883–1973) was a Scottish teacher who established an alternative school called Summerhill and wrote about the philosophies that underlie the school and its activities. A progressive educator, he was an advocate for personal freedom for children, arguing that they will learn when they're ready to, so long as they're exposed to opportunities to do so. Learning was to be encouraged, but never coerced. Summerhill was run as a democratic community, with teachers, staff, and students having an equal say in the running of the school. The school encountered criticism from some educators because of the perceived lack of actual education taking place, and also because Neill encouraged a certain amount of sexual license among staff and students.

- **Mortimer J. Adler** (1902–2001) was a perennialist who believed that knowledge is timeless and is best represented by the "great ideas" of Western civilization. He further argued against tracking some students into academic curricula and others into vocational, as he felt that denied them equal educational opportunities. Adler proposed the "great books" curriculum, which consisted largely of what he felt were the great works of the Western world, including works by Tacitus, Ptolemy, Homer, Plato, Chaucer, Dante Alighieri, Shakespeare, Galileo, Cervantes, Bacon, and others.

- **Ivan Illich** (1926–2002), a Croatian Austrian philosopher and Roman Catholic priest, critiqued public education in a book called *Deschooling Society*. He argued that education (all education, not just public education) is broken; rather than attempt to fix it, Illich said, we must dismantle it and start over. He recommended that computer-mediated, decentralized "learning webs" be used to gather together peers, to find those interested in the same subjects and activities, and to locate teachers. This recommendation was made in 1971, long before the internet existed.

Of course, where we have theorists, we must have theories. Below is a
list of ideological perspectives and educational theories that underpin
educational philosophies used by teachers of yesterday and today—and
possibly tomorrow. Again, this is not a complete list, but it's representative
of the major ideologies that underlie our educational practices. The list is
presented in alphabetical order.

- **Constructivism:** Constructivist theory proposes that individuals construct
  knowledge and meaning from real-world experiences. Thus, a constructivist
  approach to education assumes that learning is subjective and occurs as students
  are actively involved in a process of meaning and knowledge construction,
  rather than acting as passive receptors of information.

- **Essentialism:** Essentialists believe that there is a common core of knowledge
  that needs to be transmitted to students in a systematic, disciplined way. The
  emphasis here is on essential knowledge and academic rigor. Although this
  educational philosophy is similar in some ways to perennialism, essentialists
  accept the idea that the core curriculum may change as the common core of
  knowledge changes over time.

- **Idealism:** Idealism has as its central tenet the notion that ideas are the only
  true reality, the only thing worth knowing. Plato, the father of idealism,
  espoused this view in *The Republic*. An idealist educator's aim is to discover
  and develop each individual's abilities in order to better serve society. The
  curriculum tends to emphasize subject matter such as literature, history, and
  philosophy. Teaching methods focus on lecture, discussion, and—as would
  be expected of a Platonic philosophy—Socratic dialogue.

- **Perennialism:** Here, the aim of education is to ensure that students acquire
  understanding about the great ideas of Western civilization, which they do
  largely by examining the great works of that civilization. The belief is that
  these ideas are timeless and everlasting—i.e., perennial. This is reflected in
  a belief among perennialists that the great truths are constant and are presented in the great works of literature and art and in the principles of science.
  Advocates of this educational philosophy include Robert Maynard Hutchins,
  who developed the "great books" curriculum, and Mortimer Adler, who
  based his curriculum on 100 great books of Western civilization.

- **Postmodernism:** Postmodernists are skeptical of what purport to be
  authoritative statements and believe that those statements are often meant
  to empower the dominant culture while minimizing the contributions of
  other, oppressed, cultures. They believe that most canonical narratives can be
  deconstructed to expose the biases behind those narratives. A postmodernist

educator would see education as an almost revolutionary undertaking, aimed at producing students who could change the world. (A near-contemporary echo of this approach can be found in *Teaching as a Subversive Activity*, a 1969 book by Neil Postman and Charles Weingartner.)

- **Pragmatism:** A pragmatist believes that nothing is real until it is experienced and would thus—like John Dewey—champion a "learn by doing," experimentalist approach in the classroom. Pragmatists tend to favor inductive logic, which proceeds from specifics to generalities and from the parts of the whole to the whole itself. A pragmatist's classroom would normally tend to be student-centered and focused on projects, problem-solving, and collaboration.

- **Progressivism:** Progressivists believe that education should focus on the whole child, rather than on the content or the teacher, and stress that students should test ideas by active experimentation. Learning is active, not passive; it is rooted in the questions of learners that arise through experiencing the world. The learner is a problem solver, and effective teachers provide opportunities for students to learn by doing. Curriculum is derived largely from student interests and questions, and the emphasis is on *how* one comes to know as much as on what is known. This aligns the philosophy with those who argue for hands-on learning and real-world problem-solving, such as John Dewey and others.

- **Realism:** Realists believe that reality exists independent of the human mind, and that truth is what can be observed. Aristotle was a realist, a philosopher who broke with his teacher Plato's idealist philosophy. He believed that to understand an object, its ultimate form, which does not change, had to be understood. A realist curriculum would emphasize the subject matter of the physical world—science and mathematics. The teacher organizes and presents content systematically, and teaching methods focus on mastery of facts and basic skills, often through demonstration and recitation. Variants of this approach—with its emphasis on the physical world, facts, basic skills, and on demonstration and recitation—are still present in a great many classrooms.

- **Reconstructionism/Critical Theory:** This is a philosophy that emphasizes the need to address social questions, with the intent of creating a better (that is, a just and equitable) society. Reconstructionist educators focus on a curriculum that highlights social reform as the aim of education. Curriculum focuses on student experience and taking social action on real problems. This philosophy, with its goal of reforming society, is similar to postmodernism.

In spite of many generations of modern, often progressive educational thought, the approach of most US teachers (and school districts) today seems to be largely a combination of essentialism and perennialism, perhaps tempered by certain progressive tendencies and a more informed understanding of the often-diverse student population. That's not necessarily a criticism. Traditionalists would argue that perennialist and essentialist orientations have stood the test of time precisely *because* they're relatively successful and, in this age of large classes and mandatory assessments, they are effective, systematic methods that allow learning to take place, students to be assessed, and teachers to survive. Whether they're the *best* philosophies is an argument that will not be settled here.

Democratic Ideals

The democratic ideals that make up American society are reflected in both the classroom and in the society—an increasingly diverse society—in which those classrooms exist. In terms of topics covered in the DSST, that can mean you'll be expected to know something about education-related court cases and legislation. There's bound to be some overlap with civil rights issues, a topic that's also covered elsewhere. Keep in mind that civil rights issues concern more than just court mandates—although many of those mandates derived from issues we'll discuss in this section.

TIP: On the DSST—as on all multiple-choice tests—be wary of answer choices that include the words *never*, *always*, *all*, or *every*. Rarely is something *always* or *never* the case.

One of those democratic ideals is access to a free education, although a free education is by no means guaranteed in the US or elsewhere. The Constitution, after all, says nothing about education. Instead, as noted elsewhere, education is left to the states.

NOTE: In 1979, the United States signed but did not ratify the UN's International Covenant on Economic, Social and Cultural Rights (ICESCR). The treaty guarantees various rights, including the right to education. The US has opted (for over 40 years, now) *not* to ratify the treaty, largely on the grounds that multiple administrations have viewed such things as a guaranteed free education, adequate standard of living, and health, not as *rights* we wish to pledge but as *ideals*—i.e., goals that would be worth pursuing. The "right to health" clause is seen as especially troublesome, as it could be interpreted as guaranteeing a right to universal healthcare, something that is a politically polarizing in the US.

Nonetheless, the United States has always been a diverse, pluralistic one, and students are taught (from K–12) for free, with facilities and instruction funded by the federal, state, and local governments—mostly through property taxes. Americans like to think that the freedoms and human rights they espouse are reflected in US classrooms and in the methods teachers use to teach students.

One example of this is the equity for which Americans strive for in the schools. We've already discussed this concept, noting that equity differs from equality, and we used Title IX of the 1972 United States Education Amendments as one example. That section of the act prohibits sexual discrimination in federally funded school activities, including athletics: facilities must be equivalent in all respects, and that includes locker rooms, practice, and competitive facilities.

But democratic ideals in education go much further back than Title IX; they were reflected in the classrooms early on—in fact, before there really *were* classrooms. In the seventeenth century, **dame schools** were private schools taught by women, often in the home, and open to both young girls and boys. Tuition of some sort was normally charged, though often amounting to little, partly because most participants lacked economic resources; in any case, the "teacher"—often a widow or impoverished homemaker—was rarely in a position to demand more. But note that the schools were affordable and open to boys *and* girls. In some dame schools, education was fairly rigorous, considering the times; in others, the "school" acted as more of a daycare center.

America has always been a country with compulsory education laws. In fact, America had such laws *before* it was a country. The **Law of 1642**, passed in Massachusetts in that same year, required that parents and masters (that is, employers of apprentices) ensure that their children knew the principles of religion and the laws of Massachusetts. The reasoning behind the law presages a still-contemporary justification for encouraging education: the creation of good citizens. In order to be a good citizen, it was felt that citizens had to be literate; how else could they understand the laws (both secular and religious) under which they lived? This notion that literate citizens make good citizens would find currency in the works of many later educators, including Noah Webster and Horace Mann, and in the words of thought leaders from Thomas Jefferson to Eleanor Roosevelt.

Massachusetts was in the forefront of education from the country's earliest moments, and the Law of 1642 was not the last time that the colony dealt with education in a far-reaching and insightful fashion. In 1647, the colony passed the **Old Deluder Satan Act**, which required that towns of 50 families hire a schoolmaster to teach children to read and write. Towns with 100 or more families had to have a schoolmaster who could prepare children to attend Harvard College, which had been established in 1636 at Cambridge, Massachusetts. Note that Massachusetts has long been in the vanguard of educational movements. Horace Mann hailed from Franklin and eventually became Secretary of the Massachusetts State Board of Education and then a US senator. The state was also the first to create a state board of education—in 1836—and the first to enact compulsory attendance laws which, by the 1930s, had spread to all the states.

> **NOTE:** Why the Old Deluder Satan Act? As the act itself says, "It being one chief project of that old deluder, Satan, to keep men from the knowledge of the Scriptures . . . ." The act was intended to educate people so that they would not fall prey to Satan's blandishments.

Thomas Jefferson was another supporter of government-funded education. He felt that anyone could rise above his station through effort, intelligence, and diligence. As he put it, children should have the chance to receive an education "without regard to wealth, birth or other accidental condition or circumstance." The schools, in his mind, would provide the basics and would serve to sort the laborers from the intellectuals. (Note the assumption that some are meant to think, and others are meant to labor.) Like many later educators (including Webster and Mann), Jefferson believed that education was an investment in the republic: "If a nation expects to be ignorant and free in a state of civilization, it expects what never was and never will be," he said. As governor of Virginia, Jefferson offered a bill that would create such tax-supported schools, but the bill failed.

In the late 1700s, lexicographer and teacher **Noah Webster** was among the first American educators who viewed school as a vehicle for social mobility. Webster, who wrote the incredibly popular *Grammatical Institute of the English Language*, saw schools as providing an opportunity to allow those students who deserved it to rise above their current station and achieve, if not greatness, then at least a way to better themselves and achieve an improved place in society. This striving for upward mobility—and the idea that schools can help achieve that—is a recurring theme in educational thought in America and around the world: if one acquires a good education and works hard, then one can achieve success.

In the 1820s and 1830s, the **common school** movement was born, spearheaded by **Horace Mann**, who is often called "the father of American public education." Mann pushed for the development of free public schools that were open to all, as well as for standardized training for teachers. The name *common school* refers to the school's aim to serve individuals of all social classes and religions, again reflecting the American idea, encapsulated—once again—in the notion that well-educated people make good, productive citizens. Tuition was free, and the schools were funded by local taxes.

Like Webster before him, Mann felt that providing a free education was in fact an obligation of the wealthy. Mann saw that expense as an investment in the state (in this case, Massachusetts) that would be repaid by producing educated citizens who could contribute to the economy and to the peace and prosperity of both the state and the nation. It was another example of providing a path to achievement and social mobility: if one studied hard and then worked hard, one could make something of him- or herself and simultaneously contribute to society.

That path, though, was not open to everyone, at least not at first. In 1865, the Thirteenth Amendment was ratified, abolishing slavery in the recently reconstructed Union. Keep in mind that the Thirteenth Amendment truly did modify the Constitution's stance on this contentious issue, which previously had implicitly permitted slavery via the incorporation of such things as the **Three-Fifths Compromise**. That "compromise" set the "value" of a slave at three fifths that of a free white male when it came to apportioning seats for the House of Representatives.

Three years later, the Fourteenth Amendment was passed, guaranteeing that no state can abridge the rights and privileges of citizens, and noting that all persons born or naturalized in the US are citizens. Importantly, this included former slaves, which meant that any guarantees offered to citizens—including a state's guarantee of a free education—applied to African Americans, whether or not they had been slaves; if they were born here, they were citizens and therefore entitled to all the rights of citizens. This would of course have an enormous impact on issues pertaining to discrimination, in and out of school.

After the Civil War, the federal government created the **Freedmen's Bureau**, intended to help freed slaves transition into a new society. Among other things, the Freedmen's Bureau established schools for freed blacks; during the bureau's first year, more than 90,000 freed slaves were enrolled.

By 1870, there were more than 1,000 schools for freedmen in the South. They were separate schools, and surely not equal, but they *were* schools, and for the first time, former slaves and the children of former slaves were getting a formal education, one funded by taxes and prescribed by the government. This seems now like a small step, but only a few years earlier, teaching a slave to read and write had been against the law in many states; in most Southern states, anyone caught teaching a slave to read or write could be fined, imprisoned, or whipped. Things had begun to change, and perhaps it could be said that the country was beginning to live up to the American ideals it proclaimed.

NOTE: The leader of the Freedmen's Bureau was Union general Oliver O. Howard. Facing repeated difficulties with President Andrew Johnson, including clashing over Howard's plan to provide freed blacks with land for farming, the Bureau limped along until 1869, finally being completely discontinued in 1872, after the election of Ulysses S. Grant.

But it was just a beginning, and there would be many setbacks along the way. Some of those setbacks have been dealt with by the courts and the legislature.

- In 1896, the US Supreme Court determined, in *Plessy v. Ferguson*, that the use of "separate but equal" school facilities was fair. Almost 60 years later, in 1954, the Court reversed itself, declaring in *Brown v. Board of Education* that "separate but equal" facilities were in fact inherently *unequal*.

- The **Civil Rights Act of 1964** sped up desegregation in a number of ways, one of which is the fact that it allowed the federal government to control how certain funds were spent—and conditions under which those funds could be withheld. Once federal funding was tied to civil rights, the government had a powerful weapon against segregation.

- In 1969, the Supreme Court helped define students' First Amendment rights when it determined that students had a right to self-expression, in this case to protest the Vietnam War by wearing armbands. That decision, handed down in *Tinker v. Des Moines Independent Community School District*, opened the door to self-expression, reminding the American public that students (and teachers) did not "shed their constitutional rights to freedom of speech or expression at the schoolhouse gate."

- In 1974, the Court determined (in *Oliver v. Michigan State Board of Education*) that even unintentional segregation is illegal. The case involved a school district that, due to a financial shortfall, needed to lay off a large number of teachers. The least senior teachers were African Americans who had been hired largely so that the district could show a fair representation of minority races. In theory, the district did not intend to end up with a segregated teaching staff, but that would have been the result of laying off those teachers, and the Court ruled that such segregation—even if unintentional—would have been illegal.

- The theme of "unintentional segregation" continued to impact education in another 1974 decision. In *Lau v. Nichols*, Chinese American students in San Francisco brought suit against the school district, alleging that they were not receiving the help they were entitled to under Title VI of the Civil Rights Act of 1964, having been denied educational opportunities due to their limited English. The District Court argued that the school district was employing a policy applied to all students, and that they therefore had not intentionally discriminated against students with limited English proficiency. The Court of Appeals agreed, but the Supreme Court overturned the earlier decision, siding with the students and determining that the district was obliged to provide "appropriate relief."

Just how far the educational system had yet to go was made obvious almost 100 years after the establishment of the Freedmen's Bureau in a 1966 US Department of Education report entitled "**Equality of Educational Opportunity**." The report, also known as **The Coleman Report**, detailed research conducted into causes of academic achievement gaps, and noted that several factors contributed to those gaps. The major factors, said the report, were parenting influence, poverty, lack of stability, and lack of school readiness. In other words, there were (and are) groups of people who were educationally disadvantaged, largely because they are hampered by poverty and the loss of opportunity that accompanies that poverty. Note especially that one of the causes noted by the report is "lack of school readiness." Many young children in poverty are simply not prepared—physically, emotionally, socially, and intellectually—to attend school. This means that the problem, this crack in the American ideal, starts even *before* a child begins attending school; children in this position are behind from the very beginning.

NOTE: It is interesting to note that 16% of those who grow up in poverty *do* succeed. Some of that success, say researchers, can be traced to the somewhat rare presence of stable parenting, which points us back to the causes of failure listed by the Coleman Report, two of which were parenting influence and lack of stability.

Some people are simply "better resourced" than others when it comes to succeeding in school and in life. Some people lack, to use University of Pennsylvania sociologist Annette Lareau's term, the **cultural capital** that would help them succeed—the social assets that would tend to promote social mobility. These can include education, intellect, style of speech, style of dress, etc. Most educators see schools as mechanisms for providing not just knowledge, but also the cultural capital that people need in order to succeed.

To a certain extent, the democratic ideal has been reflected in increasingly integrated schools. The growing racial and ethnic diversity in student populations testifies to some sincere attempts at desegregation. However, desegregation is not the same thing as **integration**. True integration requires more than the presence of multiple racial groups in the same school. It requires, in addition, mechanisms for overcoming the achievement deficits of minority students and ways to develop positive interracial relationships in the school.

As noted, when it comes to desegregation, schools have lost ground in some instances. Even as desegregation has occurred in small towns and rural districts, segregation of schools in larger metropolitan regions has *increased*. To a certain extent, this may be due to increased housing segregation—purposeful or not—in those areas; not surprisingly, highly segregated residential patterns tend to produce highly segregated neighborhood schools. Dealing with segregated housing patterns that exist due to socioeconomic issues is a systemic problem, one not easily (or perhaps even appropriately) addressed by educators.

One of the proposed solutions to address segregation, **charter schools**, may have actually contributed to the ongoing segregation problem. A charter school is publicly funded but operates independently of the state school system in which it is located. A 2017 AP analysis concluded that charter schools were among the most heavily segregated in the country. Examining the 2014–2015 school year data, AP determined that, while 4% of public schools have student bodies that are 99% percent minority, 17% percent of charter schools are 99% minority. And of the country's almost 7,000 charter schools, more than 1,000 had minority enrollments of at least 99%. Most charters are in inner city neighborhoods, and as noted earlier, those neighborhoods are themselves often segregated, being reflective of housing patterns beyond the control of charters or any other schools.

Magnet schools, on the other hand, have proven more successful at desegregating. These themed schools—which offer curricula concentrating on such things as the arts, business, technology, or health sciences—are often set in a historically minority school. Since the themed offerings are so attractive to so many students, the result has been that many whites have opted for the magnet experience, choosing to attend those previously segregated schools. The door to desegregation has been opened simply because the school offers something they want to learn. Basically, magnet schools are an attempt to introduce market incentives into school attendance, and one result has been that districts in which magnet structures are located tend to desegregate.

The American ideal is alive in classrooms, which attempt to provide every individual with a free and appropriate public education. We have achieved a great deal in our efforts, but the fact that we're still wrestling with segregation problems—along with other equity issues—makes it obvious that American schools are still far from meeting the ideals upon which America was founded.

Social/Economic Influences

In 1937, Robert and Helen Lynd's groundbreaking study *Middletown* investigated the relationship between social class and achievement in school. The study concluded that parents recognize the importance of education for their children, but that many working-class children came to school unprepared to acquire the skills necessary for success in the classroom. Many subsequent studies have shown that there is a close relationship between social class and education in the US.

The results of the Lynds' study are unsurprising. When we measure socioeconomic status (SES), we look at occupation, education, and income; together, these denote economic, social, and occupational prestige and power. While we know that education can eventually (and positively) impact one's SES, we also know that SES can impact one's success in school.

Socioeconomic factors have always played a part in education, and from some perspectives, this was seen as a wholly natural consequence of what Herbert Spencer termed "survival of the fittest." This was Spencer's term, not Charles Darwin's, but his outlook came to be known as **social Darwinism**. In Spencer's view, people and groups of people are subject to the same laws of natural selection as are plants and animals. The idea was that the fittest individuals of each generation would survive, motivated by competition. He thought that the best people—i.e., the "fittest"—would inherit the earth and populate it with their children continuing the process of inheritance. In the classrooms of the day, social Darwinism influenced the educational mission: competition was keen, grades were posted for all to see, and the intellectual "cream" was presumed to rise to the top.

The idea was used to justify various forms of imperialism and racism. If the poor suffer, then it's because they *deserve* to suffer, and if an individual succeeds, it is because that individual *deserves* to succeed. On a large scale, this could be applied to entire races of people. Variations on this theory came and went throughout the 19th and 20th centuries with a notable and extreme example in the political policies of Nazi Germany. Natural selection, according to some, was a competition, and it was playing out as it should: one race was more suited to survival, and it was surviving at the expense of the other race(s).

In the context of education, some felt that if students performed poorly, it was because they were lazy and/or stupid; most likely their parents were also lazy and/or stupid, as were *their* parents before them. The echoes of this theory remain. Criticism of welfare and other social programs aimed at the poor or disadvantaged stem from the assertions of social Darwinism. In schools today, when people object to spending money on compensatory programs meant to compensate for generational poverty and educational disadvantage. There may yet be strains of social Darwinism remnant in today's emphasis on high-stakes exit exams, teaching marketable skills, reducing government's regulatory powers, and in offering private school vouchers.

One offshoot of the Darwinist approach to education can be found in the works of **Frederick Winslow Taylor.** Taylor was an early twentieth-century management consultant and efficiency expert who studied body movements and assigned approximations of the time necessary to complete every piece of every job. Taylor's "scientific" and managerial approach to the workplace maximized efficiency and productivity through the standardization of labor; it is from him that the education system learned about metrics, monitoring, testing, and competition.

NOTE: Frederick Winslow Taylor began as a mechanical engineer with a strong interest in improving efficiency. His book, *The Principles of Scientific Management*, was voted the most influential management book of the twentieth century in 2001, by the Fellows of the Academy of Management.

It was not that large a leap from the factory to the classroom. Taylor's "scientific management" was expanded upon by other management efficiency researchers, including Frank and Lillian Gilbreth, and to one degree or another, "Taylorism" has been present in the classroom ever since. Effective classroom managers (i.e., teachers) set up and maintain procedures, routines, rules, and standards. Management (administration) works hand-in-hand with instruction, but the effectiveness of instruction often relies on management techniques, including organizing, planning, scheduling, and dividing larger projects (papers, theses, research) into smaller, more manageable components of those projects. Teachers themselves, though they used to control much of the educational experience, have now had their jobs prescribed and delimited such that their participation has been narrowed and their input into the larger issues reduced; this division of labor is a principal of "scientific management."

Social Darwinism did not remain the dominant attitude in schools, mostly replaced by more progressive outlooks, such as those championed by Thomas Dewey. Rather than focusing on competition in schools, Dewey stressed cooperation and collaboration in the classroom. Other progressives also emphasized collaboration, project work, and exploration—guided or not—and the notion of social Darwinism lost its explicit currency.

Assimilation has traditionally been an aim (explicit or not) of the American school. In the nineteenth century, the US government forcibly relocated most Native Americans to reservations. The Bureau of Indian Affairs (BIA) attempted to "civilize" young Native Americans by assimilating them into white society and instilling what the reformers thought of as "white values." To further the education of the young Native Americans, the BIA sent many of them to boarding schools (often forcibly removing them from their parents) that emphasized reading, writing, arithmetic, and vocational training. The boarding schools were meant to eradicate tribal customs, and the students were forbidden to speak their own languages and were forced instead to use English. It was not until Congress passed the **Indian Child Welfare Act** in 1978 that Native American parents had the legal right to deny their children's placement in off-reservation schools.

The attempts at assimilation continued as waves of immigrants arrived in the US, and schools struggled to deal with the influx of English-language learners, most of whom wished to acculturate—though many of their parents may have remained insular and wedded almost exclusively to their original culture. **Acculturation** is the act of becoming part of a new culture, usually in gradual stages, and generally assuming that the minority culture retains some of its unique culture, food, and customs.

Primary schools were quite effective when it came to integrating these newcomers. The students learned English (a language that was often not spoken at home) and accumulated the "cultural capital" that was required for them to fit in; they quickly learned to speak, dress, and act like Americans. The schools were fulfilling their roles as assimilators, as Jefferson, Webster, Mann, and others had intended.

Secondary schools, though, had less impact when it came to the acculturation of the older children, often because the students were forced to leave school early. While the parents generally valued school, viewing it as a path toward socioeconomic advancement, if finances demanded it—and they often did—then the children had to leave school to help support the family. The economic environment was affecting, not for the first or last time, the educational mission.

Along the way, many recent immigrants have exhibited an impressive **cultural permeability**—the tendency (and ability) to move back and forth among cultures. In this sense, some recent immigrants and children of immigrants have found a middle ground, one which allows them to embrace their original culture while still participating in the culture of their adopted homeland.

Immigration has increased over the years since the first 19th century waves of (mostly Irish and German) immigrants arrived in the US. According to the American Immigration Council, more than 44 million immigrants resided in the US as of 2018, which is a historical high. Immigrants come from everywhere; Puerto Rican immigration to the US mainland has been continuous since the early twentieth century. (Puerto Rico, ceded to the US by Spain after the Spanish-American War, became a US Commonwealth in 1952.) Immigrants from Mexico make up the largest percentage of recent migrants, accounting in 2018 for about 25% of immigrants in the US. The next two largest groups are Indians (6%) and Chinese (5%), followed by Filipinos at 4%.

Immigrant demographics are changing, though it may take a while before the overall percentages are affected. Recently arrived immigrants are most likely to come from Asia, the Dominican Republic, the Philippines, Cuba, El Salvador, and Venezuela. In spite of the large overall concentration of

Mexican immigrants, there were actually fewer Mexican immigrants in the United States in 2017 than in 2010, representing the largest decline of all immigrant groups. As a result of immigration, fully 25% of the children in the US speak a language other than English at home.

The question of how these immigrants are to be taught speaks to the very purpose of the US educational system. Will the system follow the principles of Mann and Webster and the others, who saw Americanization as the very purpose of education? Or will the system embrace a form of multiculturalism?

While many insist that English should be the "official" language, not all agree on how best to ensure that non-English-speaking students learn to speak the language while they simultaneously navigate the bewildering customs and requirements of both an unfamiliar culture and a new system of education. Some advocate a total immersion in the new language—essentially a "sink or swim" approach in which recent immigrants attend classes full-time in which only English is spoken. Others recommend an **ESL-pullout** program, in which ESL students are removed from regular classes for a portion of the day while they receive specialized instruction in English.

The educational system is in the midst of a period of sociopolitical upheaval in which some question the legitimacy of assimilative intents, while others argue that it is the duty of the schools to help immigrants assimilate—by which they mean become Americanized. The former group sees value in a multicultural, diverse society, while the latter believes that those who arrive in America should strive to become as Americanized as possible as quickly as possible, and feel that it is the duty of the schools to aid in that effort.

Capitalism has had one of the greatest impacts on the shape and goals of American society for much of its history, and just as in the era of Taylor's "scientific management," schools (and the people that run them, fund them, and legislate them) can view the world of business as a sort of Darwinian touchstone: economic success, many feel, is an indication of competence, of just reward gained from hard work, intellectual astuteness, and dedicated effort. This view is reflected in the way schools are run. School superintendents, for example, are expected to run their districts efficiently and effectively. They are as much CEOs as they are educators. Entrusted with budgets in the millions or even billions of dollars, superintendents are expected by stakeholders, including parents and school board members, to use that money wisely—though not all agree on what "wisely" means. Thus, school leaders are working to add to the classroom skills and technologies that can prepare students for a highly technological world market; many districts are recruiting superintendents from the ranks of businesspeople; and consumer-based and for-profit models of schooling, including charter schools, voucher plans, home schooling, and more, are challenging the traditional public school monopoly.

NOTE: The notion of school vouchers is not a new one. The idea that parents should be able to receive education funds collected via taxes in the form of vouchers, which they could then use to choose their children's schools, was first suggested in 1955 by economist Milton Friedman.

There are many other examples of the socioeconomic impact on (and of) education, but one that should not be forgotten is the plight of students who are homeless—unhoused or underhoused. Known to some as "the invisible people," these are students who may not know what (or if) they will eat that day or where (or if) they will sleep that evening.

The number of homeless students is increasing. According to the National Center for Homeless Education (NCHE), during the 2017-18 school year, more than one and a half million public school students in the United States were homeless. Not surprisingly, many of them struggle in school. Remember Maslow's hierarchy: It's difficult for a student to pursue higher goals when his or her primary needs—food, shelter, safety—remain unmet. It's understandable that students might find it difficult to concentrate on Shakespeare or algebra when they may not have eaten that morning or may sleep on the streets that evening. Educators deal with a number of students with various problems, many of them quite serious. Trying to teach students who are not sure where they will sleep that night is surely among the most difficult and heartrending tasks educators face.

INTERRELATIONSHIPS BETWEEN CONTEMPORARY ISSUES AND INFLUENCES, PAST OR CURRENT, IN EDUCATION

There is a tension that exists between doing things the way they've always been done and striking out in a new direction. It's a truism that it's pointless (or worse) to continue doing something simply because that's the way it's always been done. But it's also pointless (or worse) to do something new simply because it is new. Educational approaches have changed over the years, with new ideas tempered by the experiences of the past, and past approaches informed by new developments in pedagogy, technology, and society.

This section of the DSST deals with those tensions. We'll compare traditional and progressive approaches to schooling and examine issues relating to civil rights, national and local control, the conflicts between secular and religious schools, and more.

Tradition and Progress

Tradition is strong and exerts a powerful pull on our institutions, including education. Even the length of the school year is itself a tradition of long standing. Public school "years" are usually 9–10 months long partly because the calendar was originally based on the need for children to work on farms during the summer. America was, after all, a predominantly agricultural society, and help was needed on at specific times of the year. In addition, in urban areas, wealthy (and eventually middle class) city dwellers fled the city heat whenever possible, making the three months of summer an excellent time of the year to suspend classes. The annual "summer vacation" students enjoy so much is a vestige of that agricultural and historical heritage. However, this may be changing, as traditions sometimes do. As of 2017, more than 3,000 schools in 46 states—representing about 10% of the public school population—conduct year-round schools of one sort or another.

As circumstances shift, societal factors of all types apply pressure to long-standing traditions. For example, since the founding of the country, the states have been in charge of education. Until relatively recently, the federal government had instituted a noninterventionist policy that left schools and schooling in the hands of state legislatures and state departments of education.

That changed in 1964, with the passage of the Civil Rights Act; for the first time, the federal government was intervening in educational matters in a major way. Many objected at the time and many still do, arguing that the federal government now has too much influence in what had previously been a domain of the states.

One recent example of that intervention was the unveiling of the **Common Core State Standards**, which specified what students should know at specific grade levels. Those standards were criticized as something that would do little to fix ingrained problems within the educational system, disparaged as an "unfunded mandate," and—most importantly when considering the issue of national versus local control—derided as a covert attempt to impose a national curriculum. A national curriculum would, of course, deeply erode the states' control of education.

Under the No Child Left Behind Act, the federal government could, under certain conditions, mandate that states adopt the Common Core State Standards. NCLB has been superseded by ESSA, which moderated some of those requirements; ESSA allowed the states to adopt the Common Core standards, but the federal government cannot *require* that they do so. Prior to the adoption of ESSA, though, the majority of states had adopted them.

Like much else, educational movements occur in cycles, and sometimes what is viewed as progress is actually a return to an earlier tradition. This is the case with the so-called back-to-basics movement. This is really a harkening back to the essentialist mode in which educators delivered to students a common core of knowledge that it was felt they needed to have in order to function as adults. Essentialism and back-to-basics both called for academic rigor, a reliance on what were felt to be objective facts, and respect for authority. The Common Core State Standards had much in common with essentialism, in that both presumed the existence of a body of knowledge that could be transmitted, and that mastery of this knowledge could then be assessed.

But there have always been movements associated with perspectives other than traditional essentialism. Long ago, **Benjamin Franklin** offered a relatively progressive alternative to the Latin grammar schools then relatively popular in early America. Those schools offered a strict curriculum consisting of studies in Latin and Greek, and they concentrated on the classics and on mathematics as an abstract science. Franklin challenged that tradition by establishing an **academy**, a private school in which the curriculum emphasized useful knowledge and science as well as marketable skills, such as shipbuilding, carpentry, and printing and engraving—but also included studies in Latin, Greek, and other commercially important languages, which were thought to be useful for students considering careers in business or the clergy. This was a subtle shift from the theoretical to the practical, and might (had it come to fruition, which it did not) have augmented the apprenticeship system of which Franklin himself was a product. It was not "progressive" as we use the term today, but it was an example of how one could view an educational system from an alternative perspective.

At about the same time that Franklin was proposing his academy, **Jean-Jacques Rousseau** foreshadowed later progressive movements by describing what he felt was an ideal education. Rousseau, an eighteenth-century French theorist and early Romantic, felt that children were "noble savages," untamed, but essentially virtuous, and that authoritarian schools and coercive teachers did more harm than good. He favored allowing children independence, letting their natural spontaneity and curiosity lead them to knowledge. Rousseau's educational ideal, which he wrote about in *Emile*, featured one of the first student-centered classrooms. However, Rousseau's "classroom" never existed, as his book portrays a classroom of one. Though he describes the perfect fictional education in *Emile*, he was in fact a poor teacher himself, and a man who sent his own children off to orphanages because he could not deal with raising them.

Rousseau may not have been able to realize a true student-centered classroom, but others did. One of those was **Marie Montessori**, a late-nineteenth-century Italian physician and educator who felt that children should be taught to work independently and be allowed the joy of self-discovery. As a scientist herself, she championed a "scientific" approach to learning, which entailed precise observation and measurement of the students, and for the development of new teaching methods. Although she was not above correcting children who had erred, she always said that such correction should be made gently and without anger. Her method, still in use in Montessori and similar schools today, presaged the progressive movement popular in American education until relatively recently.

Other progressives, such as John Dewey and William Heard Kilpatrick, were influenced by Rousseau and by John Locke. Even before Rousseau, Locke had argued that the purpose of education was not to make one "perfect in any one of the sciences," but to create inquisitive young scholars with open minds.

From the 1930s to the 1950s and beyond, progressivism was the watchword of education, but then that tension which we spoke of earlier reasserted itself. Traditionalists such as **Mortimer Adler** (of the "great books" curriculum) were in the forefront of a cycle that advised returning to an essentialist or perennialist viewpoint. Adler felt that the progressives had gone too far and that they had "substituted information for understanding, and science for wisdom." The progressive movement, he said, "has mistaken license for liberty, for that is what freedom is when it is unaccompanied by discipline." Adler and others felt that progressive education was creating uninformed, illiterate students who, though they felt good about themselves, actually had little reason to do so.

That "traditional" approach to education is still alive today, in one form or another. It is prevalent in many classrooms, and it forms the backbone of the "back-to-basics" and allied movements. Most standardized tests and other assessment tools owe their currency to that traditional outlook. Its detractors argue that essentialism allows students no freedom of choice; that it creates passive, unmotivated learners; and that it fails to take into account equity and diversity issues. Its defenders contend that the traditional curriculum focuses on knowledge and skills that all people should possess, thus helping to create a strong workforce and a literate society. They further note that gains in such a system are measurable, which is the only way to know if the educational system is actually doing its job.

National vs. Local Control

As we have seen, education was originally left and largely remains in the hands of the states. The Constitution itself says nothing about education, so, consistent with the Tenth Amendment's reserved powers clause, the states have taken that silence to mean that the federal government has delegated control of education to the individual states.

Common schools (discussed earlier) were an early example of local control of the schools. So local, in fact, that those schools were controlled not by the states (after all, there weren't any states at the beginning of the common school movement) but by small townships. Common schools were the ultimate in local control.

The lack of explicit provisions in the Constitution does not mean that the federal government has never had an interest—or taken a hand—in education. However, early federal agencies had little to say about how the states ran their educational facilities. The **Department of Education** was created (as a noncabinet-level agency) in 1867 to collect information about schools and to offer the states help in establishing effective school systems, but it was immediately criticized as having the potential to usurp local control of the schools and was quickly reduced to a staff of four and a budget of $15,000.

Legally speaking, that status remained until the Civil Rights Act of 1964. Among many other things, that act tied federal school funding to desegregation and other equity-minded reforms.

Shortly after that, the 1965 Elementary and Secondary Education Act (ESEA) was passed, intended to bring education into President Johnson's War on Poverty by providing funding to primary and secondary education. It was more an anti-poverty law than a civil rights one, but the two are connected; a lack of civil rights is one of the things that can result in people living at or below the poverty line.

In 2001, Congress approved a major educational reform initiative that marked a significant increase in the federal government's role in education nationwide. Signed by President George W. Bush in 2001, this was the **No Child Left Behind Act (NCLB)**, a major reform initiative. The main purpose of NCLB was to improve low-performing schools and to hold the states and school districts responsible for meeting high standards. The act, recently replaced by the **Every Student Succeeds Act (ESSA)**, marked a significant increase in the federal government's role in education.

Note that many applauded the replacement of NCLB by ESSA, feeling that the newer act restored to states their rightful control over education, allowed the states to set academic standards, and ended federal mandates on states to adopt the Common Core State Standards. Those who favored a minimum of federal intervention in an area historically left to the states saw ESSA as an end to—or at least, a reduction of—what they saw as federal interference.

NCLB and ESSA aside, the federal government's role in education is limited. There are several civil rights- or equity-related acts that impact schools, including the **Americans with Disabilities Act (ADA)**, the **Individuals with Disabilities Education Act (IDEA)**, and **Title IX of the Education Amendments Act** (which prohibits schools from discriminating based on gender). There are a few more scattered federal laws that impact education, but by and large, the federal role in education remains narrow. The US Department of Education website notes what we've already discussed: "Because of the Tenth Amendment, most education policy is decided at the state and local levels."

In fact, the main source of school revenue is not, as some might think, the federal government—or even the state government. The federal government provides about 10% of the funding, but most school revenue, over 80%, derives from local property taxes, and much of the remainder through sales taxes. Keep in mind that property taxes are determined by the market value of the structures: buildings that are worth less, being located in poorer areas, generate less money in taxes. Still, education is an expensive proposition, and about 25% of each state's budget is allocated to education.

School districts are free, of course, to generate revenue in other ways. Public schools (including charter schools, which are public) cannot charge tuition, but they can generate extra revenue via product rights, such as allowing a certain brand of soft drink to be sold on campus. Districts can charge user fees to community groups that wish to utilize school facilities, and they may also charge for participation in certain sports. Corporate sponsors can also contribute; this is different than a product-rights fee, since a corporate sponsorship may not involve any sort of product placement.

Most states sponsor a **lottery**, the proceeds of which go—or were originally intended to go—toward funding education in that state. (As of 2018, Alabama, Alaska, Hawaii, Mississippi, Nevada, and Utah do not have a state lottery.) While the original intent of the sponsors was to help finance education, over the years, some funds have been diverted to other purposes, including financing repair of roads and infrastructure, providing health care, and various forms of social welfare.

Because most education is controlled by the state, some students benefit from their place of residence more than others; the state of residence has much to do with the quality of education one receives. For example, in 2016, the state of Arizona spent less than $8,000 per pupil per year, while the state of New Jersey spent about $18,000 per pupil. The state of Utah spent the least per pupil, about $7,000, while the state of New York spent the most, almost triple that amount. Washington, D.C. spends the next greatest amount after New York, followed by Connecticut, New Jersey, and Vermont. California, which some assume spends prodigious sums on schools, actually came in near the midway mark, spending about $11,500 per student.

States do grant aid to local school districts—that's where most of that 25% portion of their budget goes—and they do so according to four different plans. The simplest is the **flat grant model**, in which a fixed amount, multiplied by the number of students, is given to the district. That model, though simple and straightforward, is also the least equitable. With this method, there is neither consideration for special programs nor for student characteristics; under this model the wealth already present within the district is also neglected. The **foundation plan** is the most common disbursement mechanism, and it guarantees a minimum annual per-student expenditure. The state pays in inverse proportion to the wealth of the local district. This plan is intended to equalize spending between wealthy and poor districts but has been criticized as having a minimum that is too low, and schools with a high percentage of low-income children suffer with this plan. With the **power-equalizing plan**, the state pays a percentage of local school expenditures based on district wealth: wealthier districts receive fewer matching state dollars, while poorer districts receive more. Finally, under the **weighted-student plan**, students are weighted in proportion to their characteristics (special needs, low income, etc.) or special programs (ESOL, vocational, etc.). This is the most complex arrangement and possibly the most equitable.

Some local funding arrangements have led to disputes and even lawsuits. *Serrano v. Priest* (1971) and *San Antonio v. Rodriquez* (1973) concerned the equitable allocation of property taxes to schools. In *Serrano*, the Court determined that allocations that created a disparity were unconstitutional, but later, in *San Antonio v. Rodriguez*, the Court ruled that it was *not* unconstitutional under the US Constitution, although it might be under the state's constitution.

Reacting to a somewhat more conservative prevailing attitude over recent years, the federal government may be scaling back its direct involvement in education, as evidenced by ESSA, which, although a federal act, is less prescriptive than the NCLB that preceded it. If so, that would tend to leave more control of education in the hands of the states and the local school districts.

Secular vs. Religious

Much of the history of education in the US began with religious schooling. The Mid-Atlantic colonies (which included New York, New Jersey, Delaware, and Pennsylvania) established **parochial** schools early on. Many of these reflected the prevailing religious sentiment in each colony. In Pennsylvania, for example, the tolerant Quakers opened schools that reflected their Quaker (Society of Friends) leanings, but the schools were open to all, including blacks and Native Americans. Settlers in New York opened schools aimed at spreading the teachings of the Reformed Church. The Puritan town schools in New England were parochial schools that stressed the Puritans' Calvinist beliefs.

Most of the parochial schools established early on emphasized a Protestant orientation, most obviously by including readings from the King James Version of the Bible in class. The Catholic inhabitants of the fledgling United States reacted by creating their own system of parochial schools.

Note that all of the early schools included daily prayer and readings from the Bible. Some might argue that the schools would therefore be in violation of the First Amendment, which prohibits the "establishment of religion," or which required, in Thomas Jefferson's memorable phrase, "separation of church and state." However, these schools were private and were in any case established *before* the Revolution and prior to the drafting of the Constitution. Thus, inclusion of biblical instruction was not illegal.

So many of the country's first educational institutions were parochial. From the tolerant Society of Friends in Pennsylvania and the rigorously dour Puritans of Massachusetts to the genteel Church of England schools in the colonial South, most of the early educational establishments in America were private schools sponsored by a church: the very definition of a parochial school.

Today, parochial schools remain a significant part of the American educational landscape. As of 2015, about 10% of all elementary and secondary school students were enrolled in private schools; about 36% of those were enrolled in Catholic schools. Some 39% of students attending private schools were enrolled in religious schools of some non-Catholic affiliation, and 24% were enrolled in nonsectarian private schools. From 2000 to 2015, private school enrollments remained steady, with only slight decreases over the years. (Private school enrollments hit a high of 11.7% in 2001/2002 and a low of 9.5% in 2011/2012. In 2015/2016, the percentage rose slightly to 10.2%.) Private schools of one sort or another serve between 5 and 6 million students in the US, and almost 80% of those students attend a religiously affiliated school. Thus, somewhere around 4.5 million students attend parochial schools in the US.

Private and parochial schools are exempt from certain state requirements, including the requirement that they must hire certified teachers. Despite that, many private schools do, in fact, require teachers to be certified. Even if they do not require state certification, they still generally require a bachelor's degree—with master's degrees and doctorates highly preferred.

However, private schools are not exempt from certain other requirements mandated by the local, state, or federal governments. For instance, such schools must still abide by laws and codes pertaining to building safety and construction, health standards, and child welfare requirements.

Private schools are *also* not exempt from compulsory attendance laws, but at one time there was a heated debate as to whether attendance at a parochial school even qualified as "attendance" under those laws. It does, but it took the Supreme Court (in 1925's *Pierce v. Society of Sisters* decision) to determine that a state's compulsory attendance laws could be met through enrollment in a private or parochial school.

Parochial schools tend to reflect a conservative educational philosophy, essentialist in nature, with a strong religious component. As we've seen, essentialism is subject-centered and argues for a common core of important knowledge—the basics or reading, writing, speaking, and computing—that must be transmitted to students. It calls for academic rigor and discipline in the classroom, which fits in well with most parochial school philosophies.

Many have the idea that a private or parochial school cannot benefit in any way from government funding, but that's not quite true. Under some circumstances, a parochial school can derive benefit from tax-funded programs, and there is a long history of Supreme Court decisions allowing aid to private or parochial schools. For example, in a 2017 case (*Trinity Lutheran Church v. Comer*), the Supreme Court determined that a religious school has the right to benefit from a state-funded playground resurfacing program.

Similarly, in *Board of Education v. Allen* (1968), the Supreme Court determined that a program requiring local school boards to loan textbooks to all public *and* private school students did not violate the establishment clause—even though the majority of those private schools were Catholic schools—because the textbooks were not religious in nature.

In recent cases, the Court has generally followed the **child benefit theory**, which says that government aid to private schools is permissible if that aid benefits the child directly, but it is not permissible if that aid primarily benefits the institution.

That theory can involve the Court in a legal and religious muddle, of course, and it seems that the Court has occasionally encountered some difficulty in making consistent decisions. Generally, though, the Supreme Court has refrained from supporting federal funding to parochial schools when the funding would substantially enhance a school's ability to provide religious education or might threaten to entangle the federal government in parochial school administration.

But when those issues can be avoided, the federal government has usually allowed certain types of federal aid to religious schools. As far back as 1930, the Court determined in *Cochran v. Louisiana State Board of*

Education that states may loan textbooks to religious schools as long as the texts are not religious in nature. In 1947, in *Everson v. Board of Education*, the Court said that the government could reimburse parents for the costs of busing their kids to parochial schools. Similarly, in 1993, the Court said in *Zobrest v. Catalina Foothills School District*, federal funds could be used to provide sign language interpreters to deaf students in parochial schools. In all those cases, the child benefit theory came into play: aid to private schools was permissible because it benefitted the child directly, rather than primarily benefitting the institution.

Of all the court cases that played a part in decisions affecting public finding of private and parochial schools, the most important may be *Lemon v. Kurtzman* (1971), because it was this case that provided the Supreme Court with a three-pronged test that it used to decide subsequent cases. The case involved the state of Pennsylvania's Nonpublic Elementary and Secondary Education Act, which allowed the state's Superintendent of Public Schools to reimburse private schools for the salaries of teachers who taught in these private schools from public textbooks and with public instructional materials. The Supreme Court ruled that the act was unconstitutional.

After that decision, the Court applied the *Lemon* test in similar cases. For laws relating to aid to a parochial or private school to be constitutional, the act or policy must

1. have been adopted for a secular purpose.
2. have a primary effect that neither advances nor inhibits religion.
3. not result in an excessive entanglement of government and religion.

Conservative justices, including Samuel Alito and Brett Kavanaugh, have criticized the *Lemon* test as ineffective in many newer, more complex establishment clause cases. Kavanaugh stated that the *Lemon* test is "not good law."

Partly because of that resurgent conservatism, it may be that the line between a parochial education and a secular one could begin to blur. Today there is strong—or at least, vocal—demand to bring the Bible back into schools. This religious revivalism has resulted in lawmakers in several states sponsoring laws that would require schools to offer elective classes on the Bible's literary and historical significance. (Those states include Alabama, Florida, Missouri, North Dakota, Virginia, and West Virginia.) That doesn't sound overtly religious, but it constitutes a narrower focus than what's allowed in today's courses on world religions. Some fear that the demand for Bible literacy will eventually evolve into more than a strictly academic examination and become instead an opportunity to proselytize, a mechanism for teaching Christian doctrine in the public-school classroom. Others say that an education focused on the Bible is exactly what is needed today.

Civil Rights

The battle over civil rights stretches as far back as the founding of the United States. Today, the term defines those rights that protect citizens from discrimination and ensure physical and mental safety. The battle for those rights reached a flashpoint in the 1950s and 1960s, but it continues today. At its core, civil rights issues go back to the 1857 decision in *Dred Scott v. Sandford*, in which the Supreme Court denied basic citizenship rights to *all* blacks, free or enslaved. Scott was a slave who sued for his family's freedom on the grounds that they had resided for an extended time in an area in which slavery was illegal. The Court found against him, not based on the merits of his claim, but based on the fact that, as a slave, he was not a citizen and therefore not entitled to sue.

In education, civil rights issues have tended to focus on acts of discrimination and on mechanisms for mitigating or prosecuting such acts. Some issues have been decided by various courts, but that doesn't mean that those decisions have been universally welcomed or accepted.

After *Dred Scott*, the next major civil rights court decision was *Plessy v. Ferguson*, the 1896 decision that "separate but equal" school facilities were fair. This allowed states to continue their practice of racially segregating schools. We can see just how unequal these separate facilities were by looking at the amount of money states spent per student and comparing the expenditures on white students to that of black students. In the 1940s, for example, school officials in Mississippi spent $52.01 annually per student in white schools, but only a little over $7.00 per student in black schools.

Plessy v. Ferguson was overturned in 1954, almost 60 years later, when the Court reversed itself, declaring in *Brown v. Board of Education of Topeka* that "separate but equal" facilities were in fact inherently unequal. Schools were ordered to desegregate, but resistance was pervasive, and desegregation, when it did occur, was a slow process. In a subsequent 1955 case (*Brown v. Board of Education II*, often referred to as *Brown II*), the Supreme Court ordered schools to be integrated "with all deliberate speed."

NOTE: With an order from the highest court in the country, it would be expected that states and school districts would be quick to comply. That was not always the case. Prince Edward County in Virginia simply *closed* all of its schools rather than desegregate. The schools remained closed for five years, and tuition benefits were provided to children to attend private schools—which had "white-only" admission policies.

Civil rights saw a watershed moment in 1957 when a federal court ordered Little Rock, Arkansas to desegregate its schools. Governor Orval Faubus refused, and mobilized the Arkansas National Guard in order to block nine African American students (known as the **Little Rock Nine**) from entering Little Rock High School. President Eisenhower responded by nationalizing the Guard, thus removing them from Faubus's command, and putting them in the service of the federal government. The Guard was able to effect entry for the students. Even then the young men and women had to walk past crowds of protesting residents, some bearing signs that read, "Race Mixing is Communist" and "Stop the Race Mixing." Once inside the school, the black students were taunted and occasionally attacked.

NOTE: Similar battles were fought in higher education. In 1962, Mississippi governor Ross Barnett personally blocked James Meredith, a 29-year-old Air Force veteran, from registering at the University of Mississippi even after the Supreme Court had ruled that he must be allowed to attend. Meredith was eventually registered and admitted, but his admission caused widespread rioting that resulted in the deaths of two people and injuries to 160 others, including 28 US Marshals that had been on-campus to protect Meredith.

Before and after the 1954 *Brown* decision, other civil rights activists campaigned, attempting to improve the lot of African Americans. Some of these activists influenced education directly, including **Booker T. Washington**. Washington was a realist who fought for the advancement of civil rights for African Americans, but was willing to compromise, although he was criticized for that willingness. Washington was president of the Tuskegee Institute, and during his tenure there, he stressed vocational training for low-level jobs for blacks, feeling that, even though they were low-level jobs, they at least provided a starting point. **W.E.B. DuBois**, who earned a doctorate at Harvard University and became a vocal and influential activist for civil rights in and out of schools, had little room in his philosophy for compromise. DuBois helped found the NAACP and wrote *The Souls of Black Folk*.

The Civil Rights Act of 1964 provided, among many other things, that all educational programs must be administered without discrimination. The relevant portions of the act are as follows: Title IV, which protects students from discrimination on the basis of race, color, sex, religion, or national origin by public elementary and secondary schools and public institutions of higher learning; Title VI, which prohibits discrimination by recipients of federal funds on the basis of race or national origin; and Title IX, which permits the federal government to intervene in pending suits that allege discrimination. (Keep in mind that Title IX of the 1964 act is not the same as Title IX of the 1972 Education Amendments Act, which said that athletic programs using federal dollars must be administered in a manner equitable to both sexes.)

The 1964 act was bolstered ten years later by the **Equal Educational Opportunities Act of 1974**, which prohibits deliberate segregation on the basis of race, color, and national origin.

In theory, the Elementary and Secondary Education Act (ESEA), signed by President Johnson in 1965, was not a civil rights act; it was economic legislation intended to provide additional resources for schools serving low-income students. The act offered grants to districts serving low-income students and created scholarships for low-income students. The act tends to get lumped into the civil rights complement of laws for two reasons: First, it did occur at the height of the civil rights movement and was signed right after the Civil Rights Act of 1964. Second, there is a significant link between poverty and civil rights (i.e., a *lack* of civil rights). A lack of civil rights, after all, can contribute to being unable to earn a good living, resulting in a population that is both deprived of its civil rights *and* forced to live in poverty.

NOTE: After race riots in several cities during the mid- to late-60s, President Lyndon Johnson established the **Kerner Commission**, the National Advisory Commission on Civil Disorders, to investigate the causes of riots in Detroit, Los Angeles, and elsewhere. The committee's report determined that the root cause of the riots was people's frustration over institutionalized racism and the lack of economic opportunity.

After the *Brown* decision(s), schools did desegregate, most of them rather quickly. The national percentage of African American students attending schools with an enrollment consisting of 90% or more minority decreased from 64% in 1969 to 33% in 1988. (It then increased again to almost 40% in 2015.)

> **NOTE:** Segregation in education was by no means resolved by the Civil Rights
> Act. As recently as May 2016, a federal judge ordered a Cleveland, Mississippi
> school district to desegregate. It had been ordered to do so, of course, in 1954,
> but a lawsuit between the district and plaintiff Diane Cowan (now Diane Cowan
> White) dragged on from 1965 until 2016, when the judge rendered his decision:
> the District must find a way to desegregate the two schools in town, or must
> build one larger school attended by both black and white students.

Students were—and are—not the only ones concerned with their civil rights. The 1968 decision in *Pickering v. Board of Education* determined that teachers (among them, high school science teacher Marvin Pickering) may voice their opinions as long as they can do so without disrupting the school's regular operation. This was viewed as a step forward in terms of teachers' civil rights.

> **NOTE:** Pickering's letter to the editor in *The Lockport Herald* criticized the school
> board's handling of the bond and tax issues with regard to building two new
> schools. In it he complained about the "totalitarianism" that was rampant at the
> schools. The letter got him fired. He spent two years working at a Campbell Soup
> factory and was then rehired after the Court found in his favor. He retired in 1997.

The civil rights movement was not *only* about discrimination against blacks. Other minorities have suffered similar effects and have had to litigate their way to something approximating a fair treatment under the law. In the 1880s, Chinese immigrants to the US were required to attend segregated schools, were usually denied citizenship, and were not allowed to own land. It took another 60 years—until the passage of the 1943 Magnuson Act— before Chinese immigrants were allowed to become citizens, and even then, the immigration quota for Chinese was set at a paltry 105 per year. It wasn't until 1952 that the **Immigration and Nationality Act of 1952** abolished direct racial barriers to immigration. (We've already discussed *Lau v. Nichols*, the case in which Chinese American students in San Francisco, California sued the school district for violating Title VI of the Civil Rights Act of 1964, denying educational opportunities due to their limited English. The case demonstrated what happens when immigrants are allowed to enter the country but are then not given the help they need to acculturate.)

While school segregation of blacks has been reduced since the 1960s, the same cannot be said of Hispanics. While *Brown* gathered headlines and converts (and vocal dissenters), not much was said about the segregation of Latino and Hispanic students.

> **NOTE:** The terms Hispanic and Latino have inconsistent definitions and are sometimes used interchangeably. Some sources cite **Hispanic** as meaning "descended from Spanish-speaking countries or is a native Spanish-speaking person" while **Latino** has been used to refer to "people from Latin America or a descendent thereof." A Brazilian is a Latino, but not a Hispanic. Spanish-speaking Mexican Americans, the largest immigrant group in the US, are Hispanic, and, if born in Mexico, are also Latino.

While Hispanics did not face laws mandating their segregation, as did blacks, many were segregated nonetheless, with the segregation being justified not on race, but on language differences. For segregated Hispanic students, the nearest thing to the *Brown* decision was *Mendez v. Westminster*, which in 1946 determined that Mexican American students could not be segregated *even on the basis of language*, since it was shown that segregation in fact slowed the students' acquisition of English.

Twenty-four years later, a federal district court decided, in *Cisneros v. Corpus Christi ISD*, that the 1954 *Brown* decision applied directly to the segregation of Mexican American schoolchildren, even though the latter segregation was **de facto** (true in fact) rather than **de jure** (true because of laws mandating it, as was the case with students in the *Brown* decision).

Despite *Mendez* and *Cisneros*, and despite the nationwide desegregation of schools since the late 1950s, the percentage of Hispanics attending segregated schools has continued to rise. In 1969, about 23% of Hispanics attended schools with a 90% or greater minority; by 2014, that number had risen to about 40%.

As is obvious from these numbers and from the earlier discussion of socio-economic status, effective education does not always extend to minority (or disadvantaged) students, despite efforts to ensure that it does. In America, the ideal of equal opportunity in education is closer than previous eras but, some argue, still not fully achieved.

Public vs. Private Schools

Since parochial schools are in fact private schools, there will be some overlap in this section with the earlier discussion of secular vs. religious schools. However, in the latter case, the content concentrated on the religious aspect of the school; this section will consider more generically the basic differences between public and private institutions.

There are some countries in which private schools are not allowed. The US has a history of private and public educational institutions, but in countries such as Cuba and North Korea, private schools simply do not exist. In general, private schools are prohibited in some countries to suppress the expression of (and knowledge about) ideologies different from those supported by the state.

About 10% of the nation's students attend a private school of one sort or another. (The majority of those attend a religiously affiliated, i.e., parochial, school.) That percentage has remained fairly steady, but since 2000 the numbers have dropped slightly. It's predicted that this drop could reverse itself over the next several years as a result of various "school choice" options, discussed below.

Although some private schools offer a traditional education, many pride themselves on their progressive or alternative approach to both curriculum and instruction. One good example is the Montessori school, which has had an enormous effect on curriculum and on the approach to the education of children (especially younger children) all over the world. Maria Montessori championed the idea that teaching should be "open-ended" and geared to the pace at which each student learns.

Another private school with a progressive methodology is the **Waldorf School**. The Waldorf curriculum is rather specific, but a few things mark the schools' progressive approach. First, teachers have a great deal of leeway concerning how the subject matter is taught. Second, Waldorf Schools argue for an interdisciplinary approach to subjects. For example, it would not be unusual for a geometry lesson to be part of a drawing or painting exercise, or for a Spanish lesson to be combined with geography or history. Rather than teaching something in isolation, this approach stresses examining subjects in relation to other subjects. In the real world, things are, after all, interconnected; a Waldorf curriculum takes advantage of that interconnectedness and uses those connections to inform and enliven the learning process. (This approach recalls John Dewey's preference for interdisciplinary teaching and to the integrated "core curriculum" of the 1930s and 1940s.)

Waldorf schools turn things a bit upside down when it comes to order of learning; they often teach functional tasks for the student's hands before all else. You'll find Waldorf first and second graders learning to read gradually and without pressure, having learned first to knit, which is useful training for hand-eye coordination and which teaches them to move their hands from left to right, crossing their physical mid-lines, a step or two ahead of their reading eyes on the page. Waldorf schools abhor specialization of student learning; they insist that every student learn everything— drama, dance, science, art, math, and athletics—all the way through high school. Students with noticeable aptitudes in a given subject are encouraged in that subject, but they are pushed just as much in the subjects that do not come naturally to them. This runs counter to the traditional essentialist perspectives. And yet, 88% of Waldorf high school graduates complete a Bachelor of Arts when the national average for BA completion is near 50%.

NOTE: The philosophy behind the Waldorf Schools came from Austrian scientist and philosopher Rudolf Steiner (1861–1925). The first Waldorf school opened in 1919 in Stuttgart, Germany, when the director of the Waldorf Astoria cigarette factory invited Steiner to become the director of a school for the children of his factory workers.

As noted earlier, private schools are exempt from certain requirements, but not from others. They must abide by health standards, for example, but they are free to design their own curricula, and they can pay teachers whatever salaries they choose. Note, though, that many private schools align their curricula to that of the public schools in order to simplify transfers, and so that the private school students can take the same state exit exams and enter college on the same terms as their public-school brethren. Private schools also do not allow—and are not required to allow—collective bargaining, and because private schools can set salaries as they wish, teachers' salaries in private schools tend to be lower than in public schools. However, many teachers prefer working in a private school, citing—among other things—a more homogenized student population, smaller class sizes, and fewer disciplinary issues.

The great majority (about 90%) of students in the US attend public schools. Unlike private schools, public educational institutions must adhere to federal and state mandates that prescribe certain actions (and proscribe others). These requirements tend to cost money, but since the public schools are funded by taxes, they can usually afford to abide by the mandates of the various government entities. Private schools, on the other hand, receive very little government aid and are free to ignore certain mandates.

Some schools—public *and* private—stress a traditional, essentialist curriculum. One such school has a pedigree stretching back to before the founding of the Unites States and was probably the first true public school in the country—Boston Latin School (BLS), founded in 1635. Although this was a public school, it stressed an education in the classics, including several years of Latin. BLS still operates, is still a public school, and still stresses a traditional curriculum with an emphasis on the classics.

Although BLS is a public school, its curriculum is similar to that of a classically oriented private academy. This is not the only example to blur the lines between private and public schools. Partly because of recent movements toward various types of "school choice" options, lines between public and private schools are becoming less distinct in general, and not simply due to the curriculum offered. In effect, there is a move toward the privatization of education.

Charter schools, for instance, are public schools. They operate under a grant (or charter) from the local school board, they do not charge tuition, and they are open to all students. They offer alternatives to regular public schools and may or may not utilize alternative teaching methodologies. Federal funds may be used to operate the school, expand successful schools, help charter schools find suitable facilities, and reward high-quality charter schools that collaborate with non-chartered public schools. Teachers at charter schools are often state-certified but may also fall under somewhat more flexible certification requirements, as established by the school's charter and state law. The best way to characterize a charter school is as an institution that is federally funded but independently run; it operates with more autonomy than a typical public school, but with somewhat less than a private school. In many states, a private school can *convert* and become a public charter school.

The first true charter school, City Academy in St. Paul, Minnesota, was established in 1992, subsequent to the 1991 passage of a law allowing the establishment of charters. By 2015, almost every state had passed laws allowing the operation of charter schools. (The holdouts as of that year were Kentucky, Montana, Nebraska, North Dakota, South Dakota, Vermont, and West Virginia.) As of 2015, almost 7,000 charter schools were in operation, serving almost 3 million students. Some areas contain many charter schools; in 2016, the New Orleans, Louisiana public education system consisted almost *entirely* of charter schools.

Though they are sometimes lumped together, there are some key differences between private schools and charter schools. Charter schools are subject to public oversight and control, and they must adhere to statewide standardized testing mandates. Charter schools must employ licensed teachers, although the charters have a bit more leeway in that area. Note that both stipulations, the licensing of teachers and the mandated standardized tests, are optional for private schools. Unlike a private school, a charter can be closed by school districts for poor academic performance.

Charter proponents point out that some students are obviously not benefitting from the standard public school system and might benefit from a charter school alternative. They further note that the best schools would undoubtedly attract both the best teachers and the brightest students. These arguments also apply to private schools.

Tuition tax credits are another possible "school choice" option. When and where available, these would allow parents to claim a tax deduction for some portion of a private school tuition. As of 2015, several states have offered "tax credit funded" scholarships that can be used to enroll students in private schools. One provision of a recent federal tax overhaul allows taxpayers to use 529 plans to pay for K–12 tuition. Previously, the law had limited those plans to savings for college education. One issue with a 529-related tax credit is that the money comes out of a savings account that parents have set up for that purpose, meaning that the parents must have money to save in the first place. A 2013 Government Accountability Office (GAO) report found that only about 3% of families participated in these plans, and that these families were—not surprisingly—among the most well-off in the country.

Educational vouchers are another "choice" option. Although the two are sometimes confused and although both are touted as promoting school choice, tax credits and voucher programs are not the same. Tax credits reward parents (and business owners) for contributing money toward educating children. Vouchers, on the other hand, are given to families by state and local governments to allow parents to choose where their children will attend school. Essentially, educational vouchers (also called **school vouchers**) are state-funded scholarships that pay for students to attend a private school rather than a public one.

Proponents argue that, given a choice, parents will send their children to the highest-performing schools; that private schools have more flexibility in staffing, budgeting, and curriculum than do public schools; and that the flexibility of private schools offers the most efficient, effective learning outcomes. Some have argued against such vouchers, fearing that they could lead to further segregation of minority and low-income students, that public schools might have their financial support reduced, and that public and private schools would end up being split along socioeconomic lines.

In a sense, school vouchers are a market-driven accommodation, a capitalist enterprise in which the schools that appeal the most to the greatest number of people would derive the greatest benefit. While there is an element of social Darwinism at play, that does not disqualify the argument. Magnet schools work from similar premises. Those are *also* an attempt to introduce market incentives into school attendance. As noted earlier, one result has been that districts in which magnet structures are located tend to desegregate, but another may be that magnet schools simply attract motivated students who are likely to perform well in an alternative educational environment simply *because* they are there by choice, studying subjects in which they're interested.

The simultaneous existence of private and public schools already argues that a certain competitive capitalistic interplay is present. The two types of schools compete for teachers and for students; thus, they indirectly compete for dollars to be used to fund their separate educational enterprises. (And in the case of federal or state funds being allocated to private schools, as is sometimes the case, that competition may in fact be much more direct. After all, funding is limited.) They also compete when it comes to academic results, as assessed by standardized tests and exit exams. The problem here is that the data are skewed, and this makes it difficult to generalize about results. Private schools claim superior standardized test scores and outcomes for their students, and the results back that up, *except* that those results aren't normalized. When one factors in sociodemographic characteristics, says a 2018 University of Virginia study, any difference in performance is eliminated. There is no evidence, say the University of Virginia researches, that private schools, "net of family background (particularly income)," are any more effective than public schools.

None of that is to say that one cannot find advantages in attending private schools—or public schools, for that matter. If one values a multicultural environment for students, for example, or favors the standard curricular approach, perhaps a public school is a better choice—not to mention tuition costs for private institutions. If, on the other hand, one can afford the tuition, values the private school experience, and has found a school with a curriculum and an approach in accord with one's values, then there's much to be said for the private school experience.

Regardless of one's position in the public versus private school debate, it's obvious that under the current administration, there is a move toward the privatization of public education. Education Secretary Betsy DeVos has said that traditional public schools are a "dead end," and she supports the expansion of voucher and similar programs that use public money for private and religious school education. How that will play out in a nation that had previously been committed to providing a free (and determinedly secular) K–12 public education to all citizens remains to be seen.

THE DEBATE CONTINUES

Education in the US has always been political, in the sense that it has been influenced by the prevailing and often contradictory political notions of the day. From the beginning, the purpose of schooling was the creation of literate citizens who could participate intelligently in the country's democracy. Further, education in the US has historically been directed toward the creation of specifically *American* citizens, and the schools have been charged—and remain so—with "Americanizing" recent arrivals to the country. The contemporary debates, though often heated and acrimonious, center on exactly how best to accomplish those objectives. However, rarely do they dispute the objectives themselves.

SUMMING IT UP

Terminology

- **Acculturation** is the act of becoming part of a new culture.
- **Assistive technologies** are equipment or products that can be used to increase, maintain, or improve the functional capabilities of children with disabilities.
- **Charter schools** are public schools operated under a charter that allows them to operate independently of the state school system.
- **Common Core State Standards** are part of a 2010 initiative that detail what students should know by the end of each school grade.
- **Common schools** began in New England, were open to all, and included a basic curriculum of reading, writing, spelling, history, geography, and arithmetic.
- **Cultural capital** refers to the social assets that would tend to promote social mobility. These can include education, intellect, style of speech, style of dress, and assets.
- **Cultural permeability** is the tendency (and ability) to move back and forth among cultures.
- **Curriculum** is the body of knowledge or activities that comprise a school's course of study. In other words, it is the planned experiences provided via instruction through which schools meet their goals and objectives.
- **Dame schools** were seventeenth-century private schools taught by a woman, often in her home, and open to both young girls and boys.
- **Educational vouchers** are given to families by state and local governments to allow parents to choose where their children will attend school.
- **Equality** presumes the identical treatment of students.
- **Equity** means "justness," which in the case of education, could require *more* than simple equality.
- A **flat grant model** is a funding model in which a fixed amount, multiplied by the number of students, is given to the district. The model, though simple and straightforward, is also the least equitable.
- A **foundation plan** is the most common disbursement mechanism, and it guarantees a minimum annual per-student expenditure. The state pays in inverse proportion to the wealth of the local district. This plan is intended to equalize spending between wealthy and poor districts.
- An **Individualized Education Program (IEP)** is a document that outlines how a special-needs student's education will be tailored to his or her needs.

- **Integration** is not the same as desegregation. Integration requires mechanisms for overcoming the achievement deficits of minority students and ways to develop positive interracial relationships in the school.
- **Magnet schools** are themed schools that offer curricula concentrating on such things as the arts, business, technology, or health sciences.
- **Mediated entry** is the practice of inducting people into a profession in supervised stages to help them learn how to apply what they've learned about their profession.
- **Sophists** were a group of itinerant teachers in ancient Greece who emphasized rhetoric and public speaking.
- A **technology gap** (or **digital divide**) is a term used to describe the advantage enjoyed by students who have ready access to technology.
- **Tuition tax credits** allow parents to claim a tax deduction for a portion of a private school tuition.
- An **unfunded mandate** is a government requirement for which adequate funding is perceived as not having been provided.
- A **weighted-student plan** is a funding plan in which students are weighted in proportion to their characteristics (special needs, low income, etc.) or special programs (ESOL, vocational, etc.). This is the most complex arrangement, and possibly the most equitable.

Philosophies and Approaches

- **Axiology** is the area of philosophy that examines values issues (morality, aesthetics, ethics, etc.) to proscribe some behaviors and prescribe others.
- **Character education** emphasizes moral and ethical development, and delves into such subjects as bullying, acceptance of those who are different than oneself, and building a sense of community.
- The **child benefit theory** states that government aid to private schools is permissible if that aid benefits the child directly but is not permissible if that aid primarily benefits the institution.
- **Constructivism** is the theory that individuals construct knowledge and meaning from real-world experiences. A constructivist approach to education assumes that learning is subjective, and it occurs as students are actively involved in a process of meaning and knowledge construction, rather than acting as passive receptors of information.
- The **core curriculum** of the 1930s and 1940s championed an integrated approach to learning that uses problem-solving as a primary method of instruction.

- An **ESL-pullout** program is one in which ESL students are removed from regular classes for a portion of the day while they receive specialized instruction in English.
- **Essentialism** is a curricular approach similar to perennialism, but essentialists believe that the "great ideas" change, and tend to favor the development of basic (i.e., essential) skills and knowledge: history, mathematics, history, science—and now, such things as computer literacy.
- **Existentialism** in education is the belief that education is about human potential and the quest for personal meaning. This often means a student-centered curriculum that focuses on creating opportunities for self-actualization.
- The **"great books" curriculum** is an example of a subject-centered, perennialist curriculum in which the great ideas of Western civilization are presumed to be representative of what is worth knowing.
- **Humanism** is a psychological perspective on curriculum arguing that curriculum must address affective issues such as self-actualization, as well as moral, aesthetic, and higher domains of thinking.
- **Idealism** is a Platonic principle that echoes Plato's view that the aim of education is to develop students' abilities and morals to serve society. It argues that *ideas* are the only true reality.
- The **new core curriculum** is an essentialist viewpoint born out of the 1980s reform movement; it's a traditionalist "core subjects" approach that requires students to experience a common body of required subjects.
- A **perennialist** is one who believes that certain ideas are perennial and deserve to be communicated to future generations. A **perennialist curriculum** could be built around the great works, which would transmit universal truths.
- **Postmodernism** is a perspective that is skeptical of what purport to be authoritative statements and believes that those statements are often meant to empower the dominant culture while minimizing the contributions of other, oppressed, cultures.
- The **power-equalizing plan** is a disbursement plan in which the state pays a percentage of local school expenditures based on district wealth: wealthier districts receive fewer matching state dollars, while poorer districts receive more.
- In education, **pragmatism** is the belief that only those things that can be experienced are real, and that reality is constantly changing. John Dewey was a progressive pragmatist.

- **Progressivism**, championed by John Dewey and his followers, is an approach to curriculum that centers on the whole child, rather than on the subject matter or the teacher. It stresses that students must test ideas by experimenting and that learning itself is rooted in the questions of learners; compared especially to perennialism and essentialism, progressivism stresses learning by doing and is an active process, rather than a passive one.
- **Realism** is an Aristotelian perspective arguing that true reality exists independent of the mind; that is, the world of physical objects is what constitutes reality.
- **Reconstructionism/Critical Theory** is a philosophy that emphasizes the need to address social questions with the intent of creating a better (that is, a more just and equitable) society. Reconstructionist educators focus on a curriculum that highlights social reform as the aim of education.
- The **relevant curriculum** emerged as part of the progressive movement of the 1930s as a reaction to criticisms that the traditional curriculum did not reflect the economic and social realities of that tumultuous period. Later reformers took up the banner in the 1960s and 1970s, offering the same criticisms.
- **SEL (social and emotional learning)** programs aim to improve students' attitudes about themselves, about others, and about school.
- **Social Darwinism** is the theory that people (and groups of people) are subject to the same evolutionary forces as plants and animals and that, motivated by competition, the "fittest" people (including students) prosper.
- A **student-based curriculum** concerns itself largely with the process of *how* a student develops his or her ability to acquire knowledge, rather than with what that knowledge is, specifically.
- A **subject-based curriculum** assumes that the subject represents a body of content we wish students to understand, or skills we wish them to possess.
- **Values-centered** educational approaches (in the 1970s) included values clarification exercises in which students studied a situation, investigated the facts, considered possible actions and consequences of the action, and then chose a value that would guide further action.

Legislation

- The **Law of 1642** required that Massachusetts parents and masters ensure that their children knew the principles of religion and the laws of Massachusetts.
- The **Old Deluder Satan Act** of 1647 required that Massachusetts towns of 50 families hire a schoolmaster to teach children to read and write and that towns of 100 families had to have a schoolmaster who could prepare children to attend Harvard College.

- The **Immigration and Nationality Act of 1952** abolished direct racial barriers to immigration.
- The **Civil Rights Act of 1964** sped up desegregation by allowing the federal government to control how certain funds were spent and conditions under which they could be withheld.
- The **1965 Elementary and Secondary Education Act (ESEA)** is a civil rights-era law that provides federal funds for schools. Its main intent was to help provide equal access to education, with the ultimate goal of reducing achievement gaps between impoverished students and wealthier ones.
- **Title IX of the 1972 Education Amendments Act** specifies that federally funded school activities must be conducted on an equitable basis, free from gender discrimination. This includes, but is not limited to, athletics.
- The **Indian Child Welfare Act** (1978) said that Native American parents had the legal right to deny their children's placement in off-reservation schools.
- **Individuals with Disabilities Education Act (IDEA)**, passed in 1990, ensures that students with disabilities are provided with a Free Appropriate Public Education, or **FAPE**.
- The **No Child Left Behind Act (NCLB)**, passed in 2001, reauthorized the Elementary and Secondary Education Act (ESEA) and included provisions applying to disadvantaged students. Most controversially, it held schools accountable for student performance and penalized underperforming schools.
- The **Every Student Succeeds Act (ESSA)** succeeded NCLB in 2015 and modified some of the provisions relating to standardized testing and measurement of schools' performance. In particular, it disallowed the mandating of the Common Core State Standards; states could no longer be forced to commit to those standards, although they could still choose to do so.

Notable Names

- **Mortimer J. Adler**, a perennialist who believed that knowledge is timeless, is best represented by the "great ideas" of Western civilization. Adler proposed the "great books" curriculum.
- **Aristotle** was a student of Plato's but argued that reality exists of *outside* of an individual's mind.
- **John Dewey** was a philosopher and educational reformer, one of the fathers of pragmatism, the idea that only that which can be experienced or observed is real, and that truth, being ever-evolving, is whatever can be shown to work. In pursuit of this experience, Dewey prescribed hands-on learning, or "learning by doing."

- **Robert Maynard Hutchins**, a perennialist and a former president of the University of Chicago, believed that the best education was one that was "calculated to develop the mind."
- **Ivan Illich** critiqued public education in a book called *Deschooling Society*. He argued that education is broken and that rather than attempt to fix it, we must dismantle it and start over.
- **Thomas Jefferson** (governor of Virginia and third president of the United States) was a supporter of government-funded education who felt that anyone could rise above his station through effort, intelligence, and diligence.
- **Horace Mann**, a Massachusetts politician and a proponent of common schools, advocated a statewide curriculum and instituted school financing through local property taxes.
- **Abraham Maslow** was an American psychologist best known for creating a **hierarchy of needs**, the theory that one's psychological health is predicated on fulfilling a series of increasingly high-level needs, and that the higher needs cannot be addressed until the basic ones are met.
- **Maria Montessori** was an Italian educator who wrote about **pedagogy**. She sought to develop new teaching methods that would transform students. She believed that one could allow children to act freely, to follow their own inclinations, and to choose and carry out their own activities at their own pace, so long as they were in an environment that was prepared to meet their needs.
- **Alexander S. Neill**, a Scottish teacher who established an alternative school called Summerhill, wrote about the philosophies that underlie the school and its activities. A progressive educator, he was an advocate for personal freedom for children.
- **Jean Piaget**, a Swiss psychologist and educational theorist, listed four stages of cognitive development in children and encouraged educators to keep those stages—and their limitations—in mind when teaching.
- **Plato** was an idealist who believed that the truth was already in the mind and simply needed to be discovered. Thus, for Plato, the purpose of education was to help students discover the universal truths that were already innately present in each person.
- **Jean-Jacque Rousseau** was an early Romantic who argued that monarchs were *not* divinely empowered to rule, and that raising virtuous, moral children was more important than concentrating on academics.
- **Socrates** championed a rigorous dialog-based approach and believed in universal truths that were valid in all places and at all times.

- **Frederick Winslow Taylor** was an early twentieth-century management consultant and efficiency expert. Taylor's approach to the workplace maximized efficiency and productivity through the standardization of labor. Over the years, the theories of "scientific management" have been applied to teaching and to the classroom.
- **Noah Webster** was a lexicographer and schoolteacher who viewed school as a vehicle for social mobility. He created a dictionary that reflected American usage, and he wrote his spelling and reading books with an eye toward the Americanization of immigrants.

Notable Court Cases

- *Plessy v. Ferguson* was the 1896 Supreme Court decision determining that the use of "separate but equal" school facilities was fair.
- In *Dred Scott v. Sandford* (1857), the Supreme Court denied basic citizenship rights to all blacks, free or enslaved.
- In *Pierce v. Society of Sisters* (1925), the Court determined that a state's compulsory attendance laws could be met through enrollment in a private or parochial school.
- The Court determined in *Cochran v. Louisiana State Board of Education* (1930) that states may loan textbooks to religious schools, as long as the texts are not religious in nature.
- In *Mendez v. Westminster* (1946), the Court determined that Mexican American students could not be segregated *even on the basis of language*, since it was shown that segregation slowed the students' acquisition of English.
- The Court said in *Everson v. Board of Education* (1947) that the government could reimburse parents for the costs of busing their kids to parochial schools.
- In 1954, *Brown v. Board of Education* overthrew *Plessy*, saying that "separate but equal" facilities were in fact inherently unequal.
- In *Board of Education v. Allen* (1968), the Supreme Court determined that a program requiring local school boards to loan textbooks to all public *and private* school students did not violate the establishment clause, even though the majority of those private schools were Catholic schools, because the textbooks were not religious in nature.
- The Court's 1968 decision in *Pickering v. Board of Education* determined that teachers may voice their opinions as long as they can do so without disrupting the school's regular operation.

- In *Tinker v. Des Moines Independent Community School District* (1969), the Court said that students (and teachers) did not "shed their constitutional rights to freedom of speech or expression at the schoolhouse gate" and determined that students had a right to self-expression, in this case to protest the Vietnam War by wearing armbands.
- In *Cisneros v. Corpus Christi ISD* (1970), the Court determined that the 1954 *Brown* decision applied directly to the segregation of Mexican American schoolchildren, even though the latter segregation was *de facto* (true in fact) rather than *de jure* (true because of laws mandating it, as was the case with students in the *Brown* decision).
- The Supreme Court ruled in *Lemon v. Kurtzman* (1971) that the state of Pennsylvania's Nonpublic Elementary and Secondary Education Act, which allowed the state's Superintendent of Public Schools to reimburse private schools for the salaries of teachers who taught in these private schools, from public textbooks and with public instructional materials, was unconstitutional. The case provided the Court with a three-pronged test that it used to decide subsequent cases involving government aid to private schools.
- In *Serrano v. Priest* (1971), the Court determined that allocating property taxes in a way that created a disparity was unconstitutional.
- The Court ruled in *San Antonio v. Rodriguez* (1973) that allocating property taxes in a way that created a disparity was *not* unconstitutional under the US Constitution but *might* be under the state's constitution.
- In *Oliver v. Michigan State Board of Education* (1974), the Court determined that even unintentional segregation is illegal.
- In *Lau v. Nichols* (1974), Chinese American students in San Francisco sued the school district, alleging that they were being denied educational opportunities due to their limited English. The Court, siding with the students, determined that the district was obliged to provide "appropriate relief."
- In *Trinity Lutheran Church v. Comer* (2017), the Supreme Court determined that a religious school had the right to benefit from a state-funded playground resurfacing program.

Chapter 4

Foundations of Education Post-Test

POST-TEST ANSWER SHEET

1. Ⓐ Ⓑ Ⓒ Ⓓ	16. Ⓐ Ⓑ Ⓒ Ⓓ	31. Ⓐ Ⓑ Ⓒ Ⓓ
2. Ⓐ Ⓑ Ⓒ Ⓓ	17. Ⓐ Ⓑ Ⓒ Ⓓ	32. Ⓐ Ⓑ Ⓒ Ⓓ
3. Ⓐ Ⓑ Ⓒ Ⓓ	18. Ⓐ Ⓑ Ⓒ Ⓓ	33. Ⓐ Ⓑ Ⓒ Ⓓ
4. Ⓐ Ⓑ Ⓒ Ⓓ	19. Ⓐ Ⓑ Ⓒ Ⓓ	34. Ⓐ Ⓑ Ⓒ Ⓓ
5. Ⓐ Ⓑ Ⓒ Ⓓ	20. Ⓐ Ⓑ Ⓒ Ⓓ	35. Ⓐ Ⓑ Ⓒ Ⓓ
6. Ⓐ Ⓑ Ⓒ Ⓓ	21. Ⓐ Ⓑ Ⓒ Ⓓ	36. Ⓐ Ⓑ Ⓒ Ⓓ
7. Ⓐ Ⓑ Ⓒ Ⓓ	22. Ⓐ Ⓑ Ⓒ Ⓓ	37. Ⓐ Ⓑ Ⓒ Ⓓ
8. Ⓐ Ⓑ Ⓒ Ⓓ	23. Ⓐ Ⓑ Ⓒ Ⓓ	38. Ⓐ Ⓑ Ⓒ Ⓓ
9. Ⓐ Ⓑ Ⓒ Ⓓ	24. Ⓐ Ⓑ Ⓒ Ⓓ	39. Ⓐ Ⓑ Ⓒ Ⓓ
10. Ⓐ Ⓑ Ⓒ Ⓓ	25. Ⓐ Ⓑ Ⓒ Ⓓ	40. Ⓐ Ⓑ Ⓒ Ⓓ
11. Ⓐ Ⓑ Ⓒ Ⓓ	26. Ⓐ Ⓑ Ⓒ Ⓓ	41. Ⓐ Ⓑ Ⓒ Ⓓ
12. Ⓐ Ⓑ Ⓒ Ⓓ	27. Ⓐ Ⓑ Ⓒ Ⓓ	42. Ⓐ Ⓑ Ⓒ Ⓓ
13. Ⓐ Ⓑ Ⓒ Ⓓ	28. Ⓐ Ⓑ Ⓒ Ⓓ	43. Ⓐ Ⓑ Ⓒ Ⓓ
14. Ⓐ Ⓑ Ⓒ Ⓓ	29. Ⓐ Ⓑ Ⓒ Ⓓ	44. Ⓐ Ⓑ Ⓒ Ⓓ
15. Ⓐ Ⓑ Ⓒ Ⓓ	30. Ⓐ Ⓑ Ⓒ Ⓓ	45. Ⓐ Ⓑ Ⓒ Ⓓ

46. Ⓐ Ⓑ Ⓒ Ⓓ   51. Ⓐ Ⓑ Ⓒ Ⓓ   56. Ⓐ Ⓑ Ⓒ Ⓓ

47. Ⓐ Ⓑ Ⓒ Ⓓ   52. Ⓐ Ⓑ Ⓒ Ⓓ   57. Ⓐ Ⓑ Ⓒ Ⓓ

48. Ⓐ Ⓑ Ⓒ Ⓓ   53. Ⓐ Ⓑ Ⓒ Ⓓ   58. Ⓐ Ⓑ Ⓒ Ⓓ

49. Ⓐ Ⓑ Ⓒ Ⓓ   54. Ⓐ Ⓑ Ⓒ Ⓓ   59. Ⓐ Ⓑ Ⓒ Ⓓ

50. Ⓐ Ⓑ Ⓒ Ⓓ   55. Ⓐ Ⓑ Ⓒ Ⓓ   60. Ⓐ Ⓑ Ⓒ Ⓓ

FOUNDATIONS OF EDUCATION POST-TEST
72 minutes—60 questions

Directions: Carefully read each of the following 60 questions. Choose the best answer to each question and fill in the corresponding circle on the answer sheet. The Answer Key and Explanations can be found following this post-test.

---

1. Which of the following statements is true?

   A. The Common Core Standards have been adopted by a minority of US states.
   B. The Common Core Standards have been nullified by most state legislatures.
   C. The Common Core Standards have been adopted by a majority of US states.
   D. The Common Core Standards have been adopted by all US states and protectorates.

2. Which country does NOT have a centralized educational system?

   A. Japan
   B. England
   C. United States
   D. France

3. Which court decision determined that "separate but equal" facilities were fair, thus allowing states to continue segregating schools?

   A. *Plessy v. Ferguson*
   B. *Loving v. Virginia*
   C. *Dred Scott v. Sanford*
   D. *Brown v. Board of Education*

4. Which of the following is true about Title IX of the United States Education Amendments?

   A. Title IX does not require that males and females have equal locker room facilities.

   B. Title IX ensures that male and female athletic programs must be identical.

   C. Title IX applies specifically to athletics and excludes activities such as band, drama, or student government.

   D. Title IX specifies that it is illegal to discriminate based on gender in any federally funded activity.

5. According to INTASC's list of professional standards or principles, one aspect of professional responsibility is that the teacher collaborates, working with others to improve his or her skills and understanding of how best to help students learn. One way the standards recommend the teacher model this behavior is by

   A. lecturing at the podium or lectern.

   B. requiring oral reports on topics of each student's choosing.

   C. encouraging the use of electronic devices or other technology.

   D. encouraging collaboration in the classroom.

6. The Civil Rights Act of 1964 provided that

   A. all after-school programs must be administered without discrimination.

   B. all educational programs supported by federal funds must be administered without discrimination.

   C. all school athletic programs supported by federal funds must be administered without gender discrimination.

   D. states could use their discretion to make block grants to fund specific programs of their choosing.

7. Which of the following statements is accurate regarding what the US Constitution says about education in America?

   A. It does not provide guidance on the matter of education.

   B. It delegated control of education to the states.

   C. It established a US Department of Education but allowed states to exercise control.

   D. It established federal control on all matters pertaining to education.

8. What was the conclusion from the groundbreaking *Middletown* study?

    A. Students perform poorly because they are inherently lazy.

    B. Many working-class children came to school unprepared to acquire the skills required for success in the classroom.

    C. When individuals suffer, it's because they deserve to suffer; if they succeed, it's because they deserve to succeed.

    D. Compensatory programs have an adverse impact on educational achievement.

9. When it came to correcting children, Marie Montessori believed that it

    A. was unnecessary; children would learn on their own that they had erred.

    B. must be firm and swift, perhaps even harsh, but completed quickly and not dragged out.

    C. was sometimes necessary but should always be done without anger.

    D. should be the result of group discussion, with the group voting on an appropriate punishment, if one were necessary.

10. Which one of the following is NOT a type of community control of schools?

    A. Small schools of choice

    B. Community control schools

    C. Charter school

    D. Community participation

11. The schools of the common school movement, which began in New England and spread rapidly, were called "common schools" because

    A. the classes were made up of multiple grades, all taught in a common room.

    B. the curriculum centered on the basics, on recitation, and on the classics of literature.

    C. they were open to children of all economic and social classes.

    D. the states, rather than the federal government, were responsible for education.

12. A seventeenth-century private school taught by a woman, in her home, and open to young girls and boys was known as a

    A. common school.
    B. magnet school.
    C. charter school.
    D. dame school.

13. What occurred as a reaction to the Protestant leanings of nineteenth-century public schools?

    A. Public schools were directed by state governments to refrain from praying or referring to the Bible.
    B. German immigrants created their own Lutheran schools.
    C. Catholic immigrants created their own system of parochial schools.
    D. The federal government sued the state governments for breaching the First Amendment.

14. Which of the following are factors used to measure socioeconomic status (SES)?

    A. Occupation, education, income
    B. Occupation, ethnicity, income
    C. Income, race, education
    D. Occupation, education, race

15. Sometimes what's viewed as progress is actually a return to an earlier tradition. Which of the following constitutes a return to an earlier tradition?

    I. The back-to-basics movement

    II. Common Core State Standards

    III. The platonic approach to education

    IV. Critical theory

    A. I and II
    B. II and III
    C. III and IV
    D. I, II, III, and IV

16. The 1968 decision rendered in *Pickering v. Board of Education* determined that teachers may speak their opinions as long as they can do so without disrupting the school's regular operation. Which of the following is an accurate description of the outcome?

   A. The determination applied only to teachers in the state of Illinois.
   B. The decision was later overturned by the Supreme Court.
   C. The ruling did not apply to teachers in private or parochial schools.
   D. It was a pyrrhic victory since Pickering was fired for speaking his mind and never regained his job.

17. What are planned experiences provided via instruction through which schools meet their goals and objectives?

   A. Curriculum
   B. Adequate Yearly Progress
   C. Individualized Education Programs
   D. Student experience

18. Which of the following statements is true regarding requirements for private and parochial schools?

   A. They do not have to follow state requirements.
   B. They are exempt from following state child welfare laws.
   C. They can deviate from state building safety and construction requirements.
   D. They are not required to hire teachers who are certified.

19. What is meant by "equity in education"?

   A. Equal access to all educational resources, opportunities, and experiences needed for success
   B. Equal treatment for all students regardless of gender, race, or disability
   C. Treating all students the same
   D. Accessibility for all students

20. Private schools are exempt from state legislation concerning which of the following?

I. Curricular content

II. Teacher salaries

III. Health standards

    A. I only
    B. I and II only
    C. III only
    D. I and III only

21. Herbert Spencer's social and educational philosophies were based on the work of

    A. Friedrich Froebel.
    B. Charles Darwin.
    C. John Dewey.
    D. Jean-Jacque Rousseau.

22. One criticism of INTASC's list professional standards for the licensing of new teachers is that the standards can be seen as requiring strict, performance-based assessments, and thereby end up

    A. controlling what and how teachers teach.
    B. excluding more progressive perspectives, such as Dewey's and Freire's.
    C. causing teachers to "teach to the test."
    D. All of the above.

23. What did the Old Deluder Satan Act of 1647 require?

    A. Churches of a certain size must provide schooling for their congregations.
    B. Towns of 50 families must hire a schoolmaster who would teach children to read and write.
    C. All citizens living within 10 miles of a town with a church must attend that church.
    D. Churches of a certain size must contribute funds to town governments.

24. The typical tenure of a school superintendent in a large school district is about

    A. 3 years.
    B. 5 years.
    C. 7 years.
    D. 10 years.

25. Which of the following contemporary practices reflects a social Darwinist perspective that continues today?

    A. Private school vouchers
    B. A reduction in government's regulatory powers
    C. An emphasis on teaching marketable skills
    D. All of the above

26. There are two main perspectives to the organization of curriculum: One is subject-based and emphasizes the subject itself as a body of content. The other is student-based, concerning itself largely with the process of how a student develops his or her ability to acquire knowledge. Most teachers find themselves using which approach?

    A. They tend to use the subject-based approach, partly because it's straightforward and objective.
    B. They use the student-based approach because the subject-matter is largely irrelevant if the students are unable to understand it.
    C. They incorporate both approaches, though they may emphasize one over the other.
    D. They incorporate both approaches in an attempt to be consistent.

27. Researchers recommend increasing teacher training dealing with gender issues and self-esteem as a way to

    A. help new teachers deal with their own personal self-esteem issues.
    B. improve educational opportunities and equity for girls and women.
    C. combat self-esteem issues partly caused by exposure to social media.
    D. help male students learn to overcome any sexist tendencies.

28. The Fourteenth Amendment to the Constitution of the United States was not specifically meant to apply to education, but it has had a great impact on education nonetheless. What is guaranteed by the Fourteenth Amendment?

    A. The right for people to be secure in their homes and not subject to unreasonable searches and seizures.
    B. Free exercise of religion or the right to assemble peaceably.
    C. Congress is granted the right to collect taxes on incomes.
    D. The rights and privileges of all citizens; all persons born (or naturalized) in the US are citizens.

29. In most states, a person can be designated a "highly qualified" teacher by doing which of the following?

    A. Acquiring a teaching certificate
    B. Obtaining a master's degree
    C. Completing a provisional internship
    D. Passing the NBPTS boards

30. Which of the following subscribed to the idea that religion should be a part of a government-supported education?

    A. Benjamin Rush
    B. Thomas Jefferson
    C. Justice Hugo Black
    D. James Madison

31. Who of the following believed that the purpose of education was to help students discover the truths that were already innately present in each person?

    A. Aristotle
    B. Socrates
    C. Plato
    D. Protagoras

32. The national educational technology plan known as *Getting Students Ready for the Twenty-First Century: Meeting the Technology Literacy Challenge* resulted in teachers and the institutions that train them, advocating for

I. computerized courseware

II. social media

III. media-rich digital presentations

IV. chat rooms

    A. I only
    B. I and III
    C. II and IV
    D. I, II, III, and IV

33. Axiology is an area of philosophy that, in an educational setting, examines values with the goal of

    A. defining appropriate and inappropriate behavior.
    B. determining who wields authority in a classroom.
    C. using the scientific method to solve problems.
    D. noting that there is no such thing as a clear definition of ethical behavior.

34. Along with the many positive effects of social media and internet use, there are also some potential negative effects. Which of the following is NOT considered one of those negative effects?

    A. An increase in self-perception of unattractiveness
    B. An inability to work in groups and collaborate with others
    C. A reduction in the ability to weigh evidence and arguments in a considered manner
    D. A failure to develop the ability to sustain focused attention

35. The Freedmen's Bureau was created after the Civil War by

    A. the Southern states.
    B. the state of Georgia.
    C. the federal government.
    D. the US Department of Education.

36. What was the purpose of Title I of the Elementary and Secondary Education Act of 1965?

    A. To enable districts to develop multicultural enrichment programs

    B. To provide funds for desegregation

    C. To provide assurance that male and female athletics were to be treated equally

    D. To improve the education of economically disadvantaged children

37. What type of curriculum approach delves into such subjects as acceptance of those who are different and building a sense of community?

    A. Core curriculum

    B. Character education

    C. Progressivism

    D. Value-centered education

38. Swiss psychologist and educational theorist Jean Piaget declared that "only education is capable of saving our societies from possible collapse, whether violent, or gradual." Which of the following is NOT one of Piaget's four stages of cognitive development?

    A. Sensorimotor

    B. Concrete operational

    C. Preoperational

    D. Neonatal

39. In the mid-1700s, lexicographer and teacher Noah Webster saw school as

    A. a vehicle for social mobility.

    B. a way to ensure that class distinctions held firmly.

    C. a means of exposing children to the great works of Western civilization.

    D. a mechanism for determining the great orators of the future.

40. Not all students have the same access to technology. The result is what's called a(n)

    A. technology gap.
    B. social media bubble.
    C. echo chamber.
    D. education gap.

41. Secondary education had limited impact on the integration into society of the first waves of immigrants to the US because

    A. a few years' schooling could not overcome generations of ethnic and cultural influences.
    B. most students dropped out of high school to go to work.
    C. most immigrant students were not allowed to attend the public schools.
    D. most of their parents felt that secondary school was unnecessary.

42. The "back-to-basics" movement would be classed largely as

    A. idealist.
    B. progressive.
    C. pragmatic.
    D. essentialist.

43. Socrates encouraged students to use critical self-examination and reflection to bring the universal truths already present in their minds to consciousness. The Socratic method consisted largely of

    A. the study of texts and treatises, combined with rote memorization.
    B. asking leading questions that forced students to think deeply about life, truth, and justice.
    C. the creation of a utopia ruled by philosopher-kings.
    D. compulsory education for men, but not for women, who were viewed as inferior to men and unable to be educated.

44. Which of the following is NOT an argument in favor of high-stakes exit testing?

    A. Curriculum offerings become less flexible.
    B. The exams show that the schools are being held accountable.
    C. The data provided by the exams can point out problems that can then be addressed.
    D. The exams focus the curriculum and ensure that key content is covered.

45. Technologies used to increase or improve the functional capabilities of students with disabilities are known as

    A. cognitive technologies.
    B. assistive technologies.
    C. distance learning technologies.
    D. educational technologies.

46. The 2010 Common Core State Standards were an example of

    A. realism.
    B. existentialism.
    C. pragmatism.
    D. modified essentialism.

47. The term "compensatory education" refers to

    A. funds meant to help promote equity between male and female athletics.
    B. educational programs that attempt to remedy the effects of environmental disadvantage.
    C. additional funds paid to teachers who take on extra classes or school-sponsored activities.
    D. after-school programs aimed at helping young mothers learn to parent.

48. School board members have to contend with the pressure of demands from a variety of groups, some of which conflict with one another. Which one of the following is typically NOT one of those groups?

    A. Teachers' associations
    B. Parents
    C. Local and state politicians
    D. Students

49. Teacher competence in the use of educational technology is

A. assumed by most undergraduate teaching programs.
B. expected of new teachers after the first year of teaching.
C. mandated by many state certification programs.
D. required by the federal government.

50. Many essentialists believe that

A. innovative teaching methods have improved performance, but at the cost of demanding much more of teachers.
B. innovative teaching methods have caused a decline in both academic performance and civility.
C. the back-to-basics movement is a misguided attempt to relive an educational "golden age" that never really existed.
D. social promotion is the best way to keep students with their cohort, thus keeping them energized and motivated.

51. Who is the chief administrative officer of a school?

A. The superintendent
B. The principal
C. The school board
D. The Regional Educational Service Agency

52. In the early 1990s, what technology was introduced into the classroom?

A. "Schools of the Air"
B. The National Program in the Use of Television in the Schools
C. Computers and the internet
D. Social media as group learning tools

53. Which of the following is one of the reasons that teaching is often not considered a profession?

A. The presence of union activities in schools
B. The absence of an agreed-upon code of ethics
C. Degree requirements
D. Adherence to a school- or district-wide dress code

54. Which one of these would NOT be used in a desegregation plan?

    A. Full-time school
    B. Magnet schools
    C. Controlled choice
    D. Involuntary busing

55. The National Commission on Excellence in Education report, *A Nation at Risk: The Imperative for Educational Reform*

    A. set off a flurry of curriculum reforms aimed at increasing students' performance in math and science.
    B. was the result of the Soviet Union's successful launch of Sputnik in 1957 and reflected America's attempts to catch up to the Soviets in the space race.
    C. was part of the impetus toward what was called the "new core curriculum," or the core subjects approach to curriculum design.
    D. assessed the methods through which the Department of Education addresses the unique needs of rural schools.

56. Schools and districts use Title I funds to provide a number of compensatory services to disadvantaged students. Which of the following services are included?

    I. Early childhood education

    II. Instructional technology

    III. Parental involvement

    IV. Guidance and counseling

    A. I and II only
    B. II and III only
    C. I, II, and IV
    D. I, II, II, and IV

57. The newest teacher education accreditation body is

   A. NCATE
   B. CAEP
   C. NCTE
   D. TEAC

58. Which of the following schools promote a curriculum where students do not specialize but learn about all subjects all the way through high school?

   A. Montessori schools
   B. Charter schools
   C. Magnet schools
   D. Waldorf schools

59. What is one criticism of a student-centered curriculum?

   A. Important academic content could get overlooked.
   B. Teachers have not been trained in this method of instruction.
   C. Students have little input into their learning experience.
   D. They are activity-centered, which makes planning difficult.

60. The Interstate New Teacher Assessment and Support Consortium (INTASC) is a consortium of state and national education organizations that work together to

   A. reform the preparation and licensing of teachers.
   B. contribute to the teacher-preparation curriculum of private colleges.
   C. work with new teachers during their first year of teaching.
   D. help accreditation agencies promulgate standards.

ANSWER KEY AND EXPLANATIONS

1. C	13. C	25. D	37. B	49. C
2. C	14. A	26. C	38. D	50. B
3. A	15. A	27. B	39. A	51. B
4. D	16. C	28. D	40. A	52. C
5. D	17. A	29. B	41. B	53. B
6. B	18. D	30. A	42. D	54. A
7. A	19. A	31. C	43. B	55. C
8. B	20. B	32. D	44. A	56. D
9. C	21. B	33. A	45. B	57. B
10. A	22. D	34. B	46. D	58. D
11. C	23. B	35. C	47. B	59. A
12. D	24. A	36. D	48. D	60. A

1. **The correct answer is C.** According to the common core state standards initiative, 41 states plus the District of Columbia, four territories, and the Department of Defense Education Activity (DoDEA) have adopted the Common Core State Standards. (Note that under ESSA, the federal government can no longer *mandate* their adoption.)

2. **The correct answer is C.** The US does not have a centralized national educational system, while the other countries listed do. Instead, while there may be some federal oversight and some shared federal funding, essentially the US has 50 different state systems.

3. **The correct answer is A.** *Plessy v. Ferguson* was the original court case in 1896 where the Court affirmed that the use of "separate but equal" facilities was fair, and thus allowed. This decision was overturned by *Brown* (choice D) almost 60 years later. In *Loving v. Virginia* (choice B), the Supreme Court determined in 1967 that state laws prohibiting interracial marriage were unconstitutional. The *Dred Scott* decision (choice C) denied citizenship (and basic rights accruing from citizenship) to all blacks—free or enslaved.

4. **The correct answer is D.** If a school activity is receiving federal funding (and most do), it is illegal to discriminate based on gender. Even private schools must abide by Title IX, if receiving federal funds. Choice A is incorrect because Title IX *does* require that male and female athletes have equal locker room facilities. Facilities must be equivalent in all respects and that includes "locker rooms, practice and competitive facilities." The programs need not be identical as choice B erroneously indicates; however, they must be equivalent. Choice C is incorrect because Title IX may have had a prominent impact on school athletics, but the law specifically prohibits discrimination in *any* federally funded school program. That not only includes athletics, but many other types of activities such as band, drama, student government, etc.

5. **The correct answer is D.** One way to model the collaborative effort recommended in the INTASC standards is by encouraging such collaboration in the classroom via teamwork, group projects, class-wide discovery exercises, and by participating in those collaborative efforts. There is a place for lecture (choice A), especially in the upper grades, but it is not a terribly effective learning modality for some students, and it generally does not encourage collaboration. Requiring oral reports from individual students (choice B) is effective in many cases, but it does not necessarily encourage collaboration. Encouraging the use of technology (choice C) is often appropriate and effective, but it does not in and of itself encourage collaboration.

6. **The correct answer is B.** The 1964 act prohibited many forms of discrimination; in fact, it made *all* discrimination in *all* programs illegal. While choice A is true, it's not the best answer because the act was not aimed specifically at after-school programs. Choice C is incorrect because it was Title IX of the Education Amendments Act of 1972 that said athletic programs using federal dollars must be administered in a manner equitable to both sexes. Choice D is incorrect because block grants were general-purpose funds from the federal government that each state could use as it wished. They were first made available in the 1980s and had no direct connection with civil rights or the Civil Rights Act of 1964.

7. **The correct answer is A.** The Constitution says nothing about education. Choice B is not the best answer because the Constitution did not explicitly delegate the matter to the states; however, its silence on the matter implies that it is one of those powers reserved to the states. Choice C is incorrect because the Department of Education was created as a noncabinet-level agency in 1867 to collect information about schools and to offer the states help in establishing effective school systems. Choice D is incorrect because matters pertaining to education are under state control, except for those issues affected by federal funding.

8. **The correct answer is B.** The 1937 *Middletown* study concluded that, while parents recognize the importance of education for their children, many working-class children came to school unprepared to acquire the skills required for success in the classroom. Choice A is a theory that continues to persist where some feel that if students perform poorly, it's because they were lazy and/or stupid; most likely their parents were also lazy and/or stupid, as were *their* parents before them. Choices C is also a belief of some, but not a conclusion reached by the study. Compensatory programs and their impact (choice D) were not a focus of the study.

9. **The correct answer is C.** Montessori thought that correction may be necessary, but it should be done without anger. She never said that it was unnecessary to correct children (choice A), though she may have agreed that there could be times when students would learn about their mistakes on their own. Montessori would never have agreed to the harsh correction in choice B, even if carried out quickly. Choice D is incorrect because Montessori did not argue for group discussions and voting on the punishment for transgressions.

10. **The correct answer is A.** Small schools of choice are limited in size and have proven effective, improving graduation rates without increasing costs, but they are not necessarily examples of community control. Community control schools (choice B) have an elected council that shares decision-making powers with the local school board. A charter school (choice C) is usually a public school run by a contracted (i.e., chartered) community group. Community participation (choice D) involves the creation of citizen advisory committees at the local school or the school board level. These councils or committees are advisory in nature, and do not wield or share decision-making powers.

11. **The correct answer is C.** The schools were open to all children—except for enslaved African American children. The statements in the other choices are all accurate, but they do not reflect the reason that the schools were called "common schools."

12. **The correct answer is D.** The dame schools were schools run from a woman's home in which children were taught the basics: reading, writing, arithmetic, and religion. Since only boys were allowed in many of the higher-level schools (including the common schools), this was often the only formal education that young girls received. Common schools (choice A) began in New England and were generally one-room schoolhouses. Magnet schools (choice B) are themed schools that offer curricula concentrating on such things as the arts, business, technology, or health sciences. Charter schools (choice C) are public schools operating under a charter that allows them to operate independently of the state school system.

13. **The correct answer is C.** The system of Catholic private schools began largely as a reaction to the perception that public schools emphasized a Protestant orientation. Choice A is incorrect because the states did not direct schools to refrain from praying or referring to the Bible. No doubt some German immigrants *did* start their own Lutheran schools, but choice B is incorrect because this was not a reaction to perceived Protestant leanings since Lutherans themselves are Protestant. Choice D is incorrect because the federal government didn't sue the states or prohibit the continued use of religion in the schools, largely because the schools were private and because there was, at the time, no federal government to file suit and no Constitution to violate.

14. **The correct answer is A.** SES is measured in terms of occupation, education, and income. It denotes economic, social, and occupational prestige and power. Neither ethnicity nor race is part of that measurement.

15. **The correct answer is A.** The back-to-basics movement (I) is basically a harkening back to the essentialist mode in which educators delivered to students a common core of knowledge that students needed to have in order to function as adults. Essentialism and back-to-basics both called for academic rigor, a reliance on what were felt to be objective facts, and respect for authority. The Common Core State Standards (II) had much in common with essentialism, in that both presumed the existence of a body of knowledge that could be transmitted, and that mastery of this knowledge could then be assessed.

16. **The correct answer is C.** The ruling did not apply to teachers in private or parochial schools. The dispute originated in Illinois (choice A), but the decision applied nationwide. The decision was never overturned by the Supreme Court (choice B). In fact, in making its final decision, the Supreme Court overturned the Illinois State Supreme Court, which had found against Pickering on appeal. The victory did have some costs: Pickering ended up spending two years working at nonteaching jobs, but he was reinstated in 1969 and retired from teaching in 1997, so it was not a pyrrhic victory (choice D).

17. **The correct answer is A.** The term *curriculum* encompasses planned experiences that occur via instruction as schools work to achieve their educational goals and objectives. Adequate Yearly Progress (choice B) is a measurement of progress that was required by the No Child Left Behind Act before it was replaced by the Every Student Succeeds Act (ESSA). An Individualized Education Program (choice C) is a document developed for children who require special education. *Student experience* (choice D) is a catch-all term that tends to be used as marketing-speak to refer to post-secondary students' overall school experience, positive or negative. If a post-secondary institution is considered as a business (and they often are), then measures of "the student experience" are tools meant to boost retention or possibly to explain a lack of retention.

18. **The correct answer is D.** Although private and parochial schools often do require that their teachers be certified, they are sometimes not required to do so; it is up to the state. Choice A is incorrect because the schools *do* have to comply with state requirements unless specifically exempted. Choices B and C are incorrect because when it comes to child welfare laws and codes pertaining to building safety and construction, the schools must follow state laws and requirements.

19. **The correct answer is A.** Equity exists when all students are provided the same opportunities for success. Providing equal treatment for all students (choice B) is not enough; some students have special needs or circumstances. Treating every student the same (choice C) assumes that they all have the same background, abilities, and needs. As one researcher has said, ". . . equality is not enough to combat hundreds of years of oppression, poverty, and disproportionality." Equity can include, but is not limited to, provision for accessibility (choice D) and accommodation of special needs.

20. **The correct answer is B.** Private schools can design their own curriculum (I) and pay whatever salaries they wish (II). They are not exempt from health standards (III), whether local, state, or federal.

21. **The correct answer is B.** Spencer championed what came to be called Social Darwinism, the idea that the fittest individuals of each generation would survive, motivated by competition. He thought that the best people—i.e., the fittest—would inherit the earth and populate it with their children, who would, of course, also be the fittest. Froebel (choice A) was a German educator who was concerned with children's unique needs. He created the concept of kindergarten. John Dewey (choice C) was a progressive who felt that students learn by doing and by following their own interests. Rousseau (choice D) was a French Romantic philosopher and writer who believed that children were essentially good; he championed the idea of developing students' character and moral sense.

22. **The correct answer is D.** Some fear that the INTASC standards might encourage an essentialist perspective that controls what and how teachers should teach, excludes more progressive perspectives, and causes teachers to simply "teach to the test."

23. **The correct answer is B.** The act (sometimes known simply as the Law of 1647) required that towns of 50 families hire a schoolmaster to teach children to read and write. Towns of 100 families must have a schoolmaster who could prepare children to attend Harvard College, which had been established in 1636 at Cambridge, MA.

24. **The correct answer is A.** In large urban districts, school superintendents don't usually last long—a little over three years. Most leave relatively quickly, citing micromanagement by the board and excessive miscommunication. The job is difficult, and superintendents are often forced to make unpopular decisions, especially when confronted by budget issues.

25. **The correct answer is D.** Private school vouchers, a reduction in government's regulatory powers, and an emphasis on teaching marketable skills all reflect a contemporary neo-conservative movement that has affected education since the 1980s, as does the competition among students and between schools that results from standardized testing.

26. **The correct answer is C.** Most teachers use both approaches, though they tend to favor one over the other.

27. **The correct answer is B.** Researchers made several recommendations for helping students deal with gender issues, including teacher training, introducing "gender-fair" curricula, and working to help counteract the decline in self-esteem that many girls experience as they become concerned with their appearance. All of the other choices are worth consideration, but they were not part of the recommendations that came out of research into student gender issues.

28. **The correct answer is D.** Part of Reconstruction after the Civil War, the amendment (adopted in 1868) essentially says that states must apply the law equally to all citizens and cannot discriminate against groups of citizens. It says, furthermore, that *everyone* born in the United States is a citizen, including former slaves, whose rights are identical and identically guaranteed. This would eventually have an enormous impact on issues pertaining to discrimination, in and out of school. Choice A describes the rights guaranteed by the Fourth Amendment, adopted in 1791. Choice B describes the rights guaranteed by the First Amendment. Choice C describes the rights guaranteed in the Sixteenth Amendment, passed in 1909 and ratified in 1913.

29. **The correct answer is B.** Obtaining a master's degree automatically makes a person a "highly qualified" teacher in most states. None of the other choices describe how an individual can become a "highly qualified" teacher. Note that NBPTS (National Board for Professional Teaching Standards) certification (choice D) is required in many states in order to receive a teaching certificate.

30. **The correct answer is A.** Physician and educator Benjamin Rush saw no conflicts among republican government and religion and wanted the Bible and Christian principles taught in schools. Thomas Jefferson (choice B), Justice Hugo Black (choice C), and James Madison (choice D) were on record as being against allowing religion to permeate the educational establishment.

31. **The correct answer is C.** Plato was an idealist who believed that the truth was already in a person's mind and simply needed to be discovered. Aristotle (choice A) was a realist who argued that reality exists of outside of an individual's mind. Plato's teacher, Socrates (choice B), championed a rigorous dialog approach and believed in universal truths that were valid in all places and at all times. Protagoras (choice D) was a sophist who taught that debate and oration used to sway audiences were the key to success and to becoming one of (or at least influencing) the ruling elite.

32. **The correct answer is D.** Having noted that technology literacy was a "national priority," the main goal of the plan was to eliminate technological illiteracy. In service of that goal, teachers and the institutions that trained them advocated for the use of tech tools, including computerized courseware, social media, media-rich presentations, and chat rooms. These mediums are known to be effective teaching and learning tools in addition to tools that most students enjoy using.

33. **The correct answer is A.** Axiology, which includes the examination of ethics and aesthetics, is the area of philosophy of that examines values issues in order to proscribe some behaviors and prescribe others. Axiology is not aimed at determining who wields authority in a classroom (choice B); legally, that is always the teacher. Pragmatists (such as John Dewey) favor the use of the scientific method (choice C) to test ideas, gaining knowledge by experiencing the results of those tests. Axiology presumes that there can be a clear definition of ethical behavior (choice D), since its aim is to make judgements about both ethics and aesthetics as a way of determining right from wrong, and helping to guide students to make ethical choices.

34. **The correct answer is B.** There is little evidence that social media and internet usage reduces students' ability to collaborate. In fact, there is some evidence indicating that such technology can *help* students learn to collaborate and to work asynchronously. The other choices reflect potential disadvantages of student involvement in social networking and internet use.

35. **The correct answer is C.** The Freedmen's Bureau, established in 1865 and intended to help the freed slaves' transition into a new society, was created by the federal government. Among other things, the Freedmen's Bureau established schools for freed blacks; during the bureau's first year, more than 90,000 freed slaves were enrolled. By 1870, there were more than 1,000 schools for freedmen in the South.

36. **The correct answer is D.** Title I was passed by Congress in 1965 and then signed by President Lyndon B. Johnson. Its purpose was to provide for the education of economically disadvantaged children. There have been state and federal funds allotted for multicultural enrichment (choice A) and for desegregation (choice B), but that was not the purpose of Title I. Title IX (1972) did not actually provide assurance that male and female athletics were to be treated "equally" (choice C). It prohibited discrimination based on sex in any program that received federal funds, and that *included* athletics. In any case, Title I was not related to that effort.

37. **The correct answer is B.** Character education places a special emphasis on moral and ethical development. This approach delves into the topics of bullying, acceptance of those who are different, and building a sense of community. A core curriculum (choice A) uses problem solving as a primary method of construction. Progressivism (choice C) centers on the whole child and stresses "learning by doing." A value-centered educational approach (choice D) focuses on building values through a process of studying a situation, investigating facts, considering possible actions and consequences of the action, and then choosing a value that would guide further action.

38. **The correct answer is D.** Piaget's four stages of cognitive development include the sensorimotor, preoperational, concrete operational, and formal operational stages. There is no neonatal stage.

39. **The correct answer is A.** Webster, who wrote the incredibly popular *Grammatical Institute of the English Language,* saw schools as providing an opportunity to allow those students who deserved it to rise above their current station and achieve, if not greatness, then at least a way to better themselves and achieve an improved place in society. Webster hoped to help erase some of those class distinctions (choice B) or at least make them more permeable. Perennialist educators such as Robert Maynard Hutchins and Mortimer Adler would, in the 1960s and beyond, argue that the aim of education is to expose students to the important works and great ideas of Western civilization (choice C). Webster's aim was not to produce great orators (choice D), although the study of rhetoric was of importance at the time.

40. **The correct answer is A.** The technology gap (also known as the "digital divide") is meant to describe the advantage enjoyed by those students who have ready access to technology. Not everyone owns a laptop or computer, and not everyone has at-home access to high-speed internet; lack of such access puts some students at a disadvantage. A social media bubble (choice B) or echo chamber (choice C) is the tendency of a social media algorithm to increasingly show you information and posts with which you already agree, and fewer and fewer posts with which you might disagree. An education gap (choice D) describes the disparity in measures of educational achievement among subgroups of students: male vs. female, rural vs. urban, etc.

41. **The correct answer is B.** In the late nineteenth and early twentieth centuries, most immigrant adolescents left school early to join the work force. Choice A is incorrect because it seems that a few years' schooling *does* tend to acculturate many students. Choice C is incorrect because immigrant children were allowed to attend school, though many left early to go to work. Choice D is incorrect because immigrant parents generally valued school, seeing it as a path toward socioeconomic advancement; however, if finances demanded it—as they often did—then the children had to leave school to help support the family.

42. The correct answer is D. Essentialism is fundamentally a subject-centered, conservative approach to education that presumes a fundamental and essential core of knowledge that needs to be transmitted to students. Essentialism is a conservative viewpoint that tends to emphasize the teacher-centered classroom, and it holds that the main purpose of education is to pass on a body of important knowledge. Idealism (choice A) has as its central belief the notion that ideas are the only true reality, and that one searches for truth by utilizing a consciously reasoned process to uncover and develop one's abilities. Progressivism (choice B) centers on the whole child, rather than on the subject matter or the teacher. The philosophy stresses that students must test ideas by experimenting, and that learning itself is rooted in the questions of learners. Compared especially to perennialism and essentialism, progressivism stresses learning by doing and is an active process, rather than a passive one. Pragmatism (choice C) in education involves the notion that only that which can be experienced or observed is real, and that truth, being ever-evolving, is whatever works.

43. The correct answer is B. The Socratic dialog, as it is known, is an educational method in which the teacher leads the student not by providing answers, but by asking questions designed to make the student find the answer(s) on his or her own. The study of texts, combined with rote memorization (choice A), is a feature of many early educational approaches, but it is not Socratic. Plato envisioned a utopia ruled by philosopher-kings (choice C), which incorporated an idealized society in which educators sorted people into ability groups and then educated them based on their perceived intellectual abilities and potential. The Socratic method did not involve or address the supposed intellectual inferiority of women (choice D). Aristotle, a student of Plato and the tutor of Alexander the Great, was a proponent of compulsory education for men, but not for women, whom he deemed intellectually inferior to men.

44. The correct answer is A. The decreased curricular flexibility is an argument *against* such testing. The other choices all reflect arguments in favor of high-stakes exit exams.

45. **The correct answer is B.** Assistive technologies are equipment or products (commercial or customized) that can be used to increase, maintain, or improve the functional capabilities of children with disabilities. Assistive technologies are closely related to adaptive technologies, which the US government defines as "External support that can be used to enhance a person's ability to function within his or her environment, such as advanced voice recognition systems, Braille computer displays, and text-to-speech programs." Cognitive technologies (choice A) would be a broad category that includes anything that enhances or relates to cognitive function. Distance learning technologies (choice C) are those technologies and tools that involve or enable course-taking or educational participation at a distance. Educational technologies (choice D) are any technologies used in the classroom in the delivery or assessment of instruction. This is a broad term that encompasses almost every tool brought into the classroom and used to further teaching: radio, television, film projectors, VCRs, whiteboards, and more. Almost every tool, including the pencil and the chalkboard, is a type of technology.

46. **The correct answer is D.** The Common Core State Standards reflected an updated essentialist outlook that identifies mainly language arts (English) and mathematics as subjects for which mastery is required in order to be successful. Realism (choice A) is the Aristotelian idea that reality exists independent of the human mind, and that logic can (and must) be used to understand the world. Thus, a realistic educational approach emphasizes the physical world and demands the mastery of basic skills and critical thinking, which requires a standardized curriculum. Existentialist educators (choice B) believe that the nature of reality is subjective, and that classroom subject matter should be a matter of personal choice. Thus, existentialist educators tend to oppose measuring or tracking students according to standardized mechanisms; instead, they believe that the educational experience should focus on students' self-direction and self-actualization. Pragmatism (choice C) is the philosophy that only those things that are experienced are truly real, a view that John Dewey built into his progressive curriculum by emphasizing social experience and adaptation to the student's environment—and to each other.

47. The correct answer is B. Compensatory programs are those that attempt to undo the damage done by years, or even generations, of disadvantage. Funds used to promote equity between male and female athletics (choice A) are provided under Title IX. There are often additional stipends for teachers who take on extra roles in or after school (choice C), but those are generally supplied by the school or district, and this is not known as compensatory education. Some schools and districts do offer programs for young mothers (choice D), but these are not necessarily part of compensatory education.

48. The correct answer is D. Although students, in rare cases, might address a school board meeting, they are seldom in a position to put pressure on the board itself. Schools boards are often under pressure from teachers' associations (choice A), parents (choice B), and politicians (choice C). Politicians often have input into funding decisions.

49. The correct answer is C. Most state certification and professional teacher accreditation programs require the teacher to have shown competence in various forms of educational technology. Choice A is incorrect because competence is not assumed by undergraduate programs; courses in the subject are required in order to earn a degree and credential. Choice B is incorrect because in the public schools, administrators and school boards expect new teachers to enter the profession *already* competent in educational technology; it is not a skill one is expected to gain after having taught for a year. Competence in educational technology is not directly mandated by the federal government (choice D), although the government does supply resources useful for learning about and integrating technology in the classroom.

50. **The correct answer is B.** Essentialists believe the school's main function is to maintain the achievements of human civilization by transmitting them to students in a carefully sequenced curriculum that stresses essential skills and knowledge. Most innovative methods, they believe, have misfired badly, often doing more harm than good. Essentialists do not believe that performance has improved (choice A), though they may agree that teachers' time and effort is being used ineffectively and inefficiently. Most essentialists would favor a "back-to-basics" (choice C) approach to curriculum. Essentialists charge that social promotion (choice D), advancing students to the next grade in order to keep them with their cohort even if they have not mastered the required skills, is further eroding academic standards.

51. **The correct answer is B.** The principal runs a specific school—often referred to simply as a "building"—and is in effect the chief administrative officer of the school. The superintendent (choice A) runs the district, much like a company's chief executive officer runs a company. The school board (choice C) has a great deal of input, but no actual authority except during a board meeting. A RESA (choice D) is an autonomous, tax-supported public school district positioned in between the local board and the state department of education. It is the only educational entity with full access to public schools to ensure implementation of core educational services and programs to develop and maintain shared resources.

52. **The correct answer is C.** In the 1990s, computers and the internet began making their way into classrooms other than just science and tech-related classes. Tim Berners-Lee and Robert Cilia developed the prototype of the World Wide Web in 1990, and Marc Andreesen and Eric Bina developed the first commercial browser, Mosaic, in 1993. "Schools of The Air" (choice A) debuted in the 1930s and brought cultural and music-appreciation programs into classrooms. The National Program in the Use of Television in the Schools (choice B) was initiated in 1957. The use of social media in schools (choice D) has proven to be both useful and problematic, but in any case, the first commercially successful social networking site was probably Friendster, which debuted in 2002, followed by Myspace in 2003. (Facebook was late to the party, as it wasn't introduced until 2004.)

53. **The correct answer is B.** The public has a certain perception with regard to the hallmarks of professionalism. The fact that the teaching profession does not have an agreed-upon code of ethics to abide by is a distinct disadvantage. While the AFT and NEA each promulgate such a code (or in the case of the AFT, the *need* for such a code), teachers are not required to agree to it, nor are they disciplined by their own organization for failing to abide by it. This contributes to the impression that teaching is not a profession.

54. **The correct answer is A.** Full-time school (in which a school is open all year, and students attend three out of four quarters) might be considered for a number of reasons (more efficient use of resources, staffing, and others), but it is not normally something that would contribute to desegregation the way the other choices would.

55. **The correct answer is C.** The Commission's report, issued in 1983, described students as being inadequately prepared for both work and college, and recommended a core subjects approach that was essentialist in nature, concentrating on "the basics" and requiring students to experience a common body of required subjects. What set off a flurry of reforms aimed at improving science and math education (choice A) was the Soviet Union's successful launch of Sputnik in 1957 (choice B). The report that assessed the methods through which the Department of Education addresses the needs of rural schools (choice D) was the so-called Rural Report, released in 2018 as required by the Every Student Succeeds Act (ESSA).

56. **The correct answer is D.** Early childhood education (I), instructional technology (II), parental involvement (III), and guidance and counseling (IV) are all funded by Title I, as are bilingual education, dropout prevention, and several others.

57. **The correct answer is B.** The Council for the Accreditation of Educator Preparation (CAEP) was fully established in 2013 and has adopted standards that attempt to determine which teacher-education programs comply with national standards. The National Council for the Accreditation of Teacher Education (choice A) and the Teacher Education Accreditation Council (choice D) are predecessors to CAEP. The NCTE (choice C) is the National Council of Teachers of English.

58. **The correct answer is D.** Waldorf schools abhor specialization of student learning and insist that every student learn everything—drama, dance, science, art, math, and athletics—all the way through high school. Students with noticeable aptitudes in a given subject are encouraged in that subject, but they are pushed just as much in the subjects that do not come naturally to them. In a Montessori school (choice A), the curriculum is open-ended, and each student learns at his or her own pace. Charter schools (choice B) are public schools set up under community control to provide alternative visions of schooling; they allow for more autonomy from state and district regulations and in designing the curriculum. Magnet schools (choice C) are public schools with an emphasis on specialized curricula; these are often set up in an effort to attract students throughout a school district, sometimes in an effort to encourage desegregation.

59. **The correct answer is A.** With various forms of student-centered curricula, it's possible to overlook important content. Choice B is incorrect because most teachers have been trained in multiple approaches to curriculum; in any case, lack of training could be overcome by diligent preparation, especially if teacher mentoring and guidance is available. The opposite of choice C is true. Students have a great deal of input in a student-centered curriculum. Not all student-centered curriculum approaches are activity-centered as choice D indicates, and many activity-centered approaches are perfectly amenable to planning. However, some proponents of activity-centered curricula believed that, since teachers cannot anticipate the interests and needs of children, a preplanned curriculum is impossible.

60. **The correct answer is A.** The goal of INTASC is to help state education agencies prepare and license teachers. INTASC also works to further the ongoing professional development of teachers. INTASC does not directly contribute to curriculum (choice B), and to the extent that its standards *are* reflected in curriculum, their effects are not limited to private colleges. INTASC does not work with new teachers (choice C), except in terms of ongoing professional development once the teachers are licensed. INTASC does not work directly with accreditation agencies to help those agencies promulgate standards (choice D), although INTASC does promulgate its own widely accepted set of standards.

Like what you see? Get unlimited access to Peterson's full catalog of DSST practice tests, instructional videos, flashcards, and more for **75% off the first month!** Go to **www.petersons.com/testprep/dsst** and use coupon code **DSST2020** at checkout. Offer expires July 1, 2021.

CPSIA information can be obtained
at www.ICGtesting.com
Printed in the USA
JSHW041312190722
28277JS00007B/138